All
the
Wild
Hungers

ALSO BY KAREN BABINE

Water and What We Know: Following the Roots of a Northern Life

All
the
Wild
Hungers

A Season of Cooking and Cancer

KAREN BABINE

MILKWEED EDITIONS

Published 2019 by Milkweed Editions
Printed in Canada
Cover design by Mary Austin Speaker
Cover art: cabbage and apple by Nadezhda Shoshina;
lemon by Ekaterina Arkhangelskaia | Dreamstime.com
19 20 21 22 23 5 4 3 2 1
First Edition

Milkweed Editions, an independent nonprofit publisher, gratefully acknowledges sustaining support from the Jerome Foundation; the McKnight Foundation; the National Endowment for the Arts; the Target Foundation; and other generous contributions from foundations, corporations, and individuals. Also, this activity is made possible by the voters of Minnesota through a Minnesota State Arts Board Operating Support grant, thanks to a legislative appropriation from the arts and cultural heritage fund, and a grant from Wells Fargo. For a full listing of Milkweed Editions supporters, please visit milkweed.org.

Library of Congress Cataloging-in-Publication Data

Names: Babine, Karen, 1978- author.
Title: All the wild hungers : a season of cooking and cancer / Karen Babine.
Description: First edition. | Minneapolis, Minnesota : Milkweed Editions, [2019].
Identifiers: LCCN 2018023757 (print) | LCCN 2018035815 (ebook) | ISBN 9781571319838 (ebook) | ISBN 9781571313720 | ISBN 9781571313720 q(paperback : qalk. paper)
Subjects: LCSH: Babine, Karen, 1978- | Babine, Karen, 1978---Family. | Children of cancer patients--United States--Biography. | Authors, American--21st century--Biography. | Cooking--Anecdotes. | LCGFT: Autobiographies. | Essays.
Classification: LCC RC265.6.B42 (ebook) | LCC RC265.6.B42 A3 2019 (print) |
         DDC 618.92/994--dc23
         LC record available at https://lccn.loc.gov/2018023757

For my mother

All
the
Wild
Hungers

I

IT STARTED THIS WAY: in early October, my mother's doctor asked her if she felt pregnant, if she had bladder issues, digestive problems, clothes not fitting right. My mother's immediate answer was *no*—but she went home and thought about where her weight was sitting, what she hadn't been able to exercise away, the constant constipation, the bloating she chalked up to eating badly while traveling, and she realized she did feel four months pregnant. I tried not to call the tumor her *cancer baby*, at least not out loud.

My middle sister is currently fourteen weeks pregnant with her third child and the family is ecstatic with joy. Six years ago, when my sister was pregnant with my niece, she sent a text that she and the dog "were taking the Apple for a walk." We thought it was cute, as we are a small, tightly knit family that likes to think in Proper Nouns, to name things, to put even the most quotidian into its proper context. My sister is pregnant with a Lemon this week, Week 14, and this is amusing. My mother's uterine tumor, the size of a cabbage, is Week 30, and this is terrifying. Three years ago, my nephew was born at Week 36, but he was the size of that cancerous cabbage. There are patterns emerging here that I do not like.

We learn that my mother's is a childhood cancer called embryonal rhabdomyosarcoma and they tell us it appears only in children under the age of ten, not in sixty-five-year-old grandmothers, and I keep thinking of embryos, about the physical and emotional dangers of pregnancy, the risks of birth in a country that boasts the largest maternal death rate among developed nations, that women of color are at even more risk from dying as a result of pregnancy and childbirth, and that the risk transcends economic status. Serena Williams's blood clots were not immediately taken seriously after she gave birth, leading to nearly deadly results; activist Erica Garner suffered a heart attack and passed away three months after giving birth. I keep thinking about what is inside us that never goes away, love and fear, scars that are emotional and physical. The long length of my mother's abdominal scar is a bright, rich eggplant purple, necessary so the surgeon could deliver her uterus and tumor intact; her own mother's identical hysterectomy scar had long ago faded to white, an ectopic pregnancy in 1952 that nearly caused her to bleed to death. The lines that tie us together are written into our skin, into our cells, the potential destruction of a family present in its creation.

2

ONCE UPON A TIME, a girl who loved chocolate wanted to become a teacher. Her parents were both teachers, each the first in their rural farm families to attend and graduate from a four-year college. The girl loved music and believed chocolate was the answer to any question she had. The woman who loved chocolate made children the work of her life, spending the last fifteen years of her career teaching fourth grade. She would say, *They're old enough to read and young enough to still listen.* When Christmas would come around, the children remembered she loved chocolate more than anything, wrapping up Hershey's rather than another World's Greatest Teacher coffee mug. She would warn them that *there's no fun in fourth grade* and they would look up, startled, and say, *But this is fun!* and laugh at the twinkle in her bright blue eyes. I wonder what she would see now if she were still in her classroom, looking out at those ten-year-old faces. I wonder which stories this teacher would read to her students now, the lights dimmed after lunch. Would the woman who loved chocolate see old tales in their faces, the dark stories, the ones where the women are the danger, the absent and dead mothers, murderous stepmothers, evil disguised as grandmothers, the stories where witches lure children closer with houses made of candy and gingerbread, where stepmother-witches offer poisoned apples, where tiny bottles labeled Drink Me and cakes labeled Eat Me send us to places we never expected to go?

3

MY BELOVED ORANGE LE Creuset cast-iron skillet, size 23, was the first of my cast iron collection, and her origin story goes like this: I saw the bright enamel on a thrift store shelf more than a year before the cancer, before cast iron would become a thrill, before my mother's palliative doctor would remind her that "pleasure is important." The skillet was buried under other cookware, and when I flipped it over, I ran my finger over the gunk on the bottom of the pan, as if I could read the letters there by touch. *Who brings Le Creuset to a thrift store?* I took it home for $7.99, scrubbed it with coarse salt and oil, then set to season it with the help of Google because I had no idea what to do with cast iron. That night, I made a frittata that was mostly edible. The skillet's name became Agnes, named for romance novelist Jennifer Crusie's heroine in *Agnes and the Hitman*, a cook who tends to defend herself with her nonstick skillet as hijinks ensue.

Halloween came a week after my mother was diagnosed, two days before she was scheduled for surgery because nobody wanted to wait, before the Halloween pumpkin language turned into Thanksgiving pies that would herald the beginning of chemotherapy, before I lost myself in the food metaphors of cancer, before I started hunting all that bright, expensive cookware in my local thrift stores, before the quest for cast iron became an obsession to keep me grounded, before my orange Le Creuset skillet became an explosion of color and delight that gave me a dedicated purpose, before I began cooking for my mother against the feeling that food had become something to be feared.

Agnes is the color of orange not found in nature, not citrus or pumpkin or persimmon. She is cheap boxed macaroni and cheese. She is the color of warning, of flame and blaze orange, that keeps our hunter friends safe in the woods on these chilly days. She is the artificial-looking color of the gerbera daisies delivered to my mother's hospital room the day a three-pound, sixteen-centimeter embryonal rhabdomyosarcoma tumor is excavated with my mother's uterus. It is a cancer so rare in adults that I contact a high school friend who is a doctor at the Mayo Clinic for advice and he connects us with a sarcoma specialist there. My mother could have chosen to do her treatment at Mayo, but she decided on the University of Minnesota, since it is so much closer to home, and we begin a collaboration with their sarcoma specialist. We learn that if my mother were my niece's age, the doctors would know what to do, but she is sixty-five, and they must extrapolate a treatment plan from what they would give a child. A three-week cycle of chemotherapy, they decide—three drugs given on Day 1, one on Day 8, one on Day 15. Even then, they are still guessing that this is the right path. We learn that she is given a lower dose of this cocktail, because children can tolerate stronger chemotherapy, which seems counterintuitive.

What they do say is this: my mother is cancer free after this surgery, but they are prescribing aggressive chemotherapy because if she does not do chemo, there is a 70 percent chance the cancer will come back, and if it does, she has a 40 percent chance of survival. With chemo, she has a 90 percent chance of survival if it returns. She chooses chemo. Nobody argues.

4

WHEN OCTOBER DAYS GROW short and opaque and the dense of sky presses down like the palm of a hand, I crave cabbage, the resistance of green steamed just enough to bite, Brussels sprouts cut in half and sautéed in butter and olive oil. In the celadon spring, I always want colcannon. In these early days of cancer, my family—my parents, two sisters, brother-in-law, niece, and nephew—institute a weekly family dinner to alleviate the fear in our bellies over what is happening to our mother. We are a family that crowds three adult daughters into the consultation room with our parents and our mother's doctors, prompting one doctor to look from me to my youngest sister and back again and ask if we are twins, and we laugh and say there are four years between us. Our family is very close, both geographically and emotionally, and this colors our reactions to the world around us. Because we live within a ten-mile radius, it is common for us to toss out impromptu invitations, so when we think about making each moment count, we realize that we have not changed much about the way we are with each other. Cancer simply requires that we articulate ourselves differently, reorienting our language as we become intimately aware of the words we use. We come to understand the idea of "cancer-adjusted normal," that what might have constituted a bad day a year ago is actually a truly good day today. We don't ask *how are you doing?* anymore—we ask *how is today?*

On one of these nights full of family and color and sound, I pull out Estelle, my vintage Le Creuset cast-iron Dutch oven, rescued from a thrift store about the time my mother was diagnosed, and I realize that Estelle is Week 14 Lemon Yellow and I'm seeing pregnancy and cancer and food everywhere. Tonight, I want the bright of braised red cabbage against that pale-yellow enamel, the bite of vinegar and sharp apples, because today is a day that stings the inside of my skin like balsamic breathed too deeply. I sauté the sharpness of two thinly sliced onions down to sweetness, then add fennel seeds until they warm the room. Three Granny Smith apples, cut into chunks, are stirred gently into the onion, and then I turn to the red cabbage, which will be chopped and added to the pot with enough balsamic vinegar to braise over the course of an hour. I refuse to think of pathology as I slice harder than necessary through dark purple and white, the hidden patterns and swirls in the packed leaves too beautiful to be accidental.

5

MY MOTHER'S SURGEON SAYS that the margins and lymph nodes are clear, but skepticism lingers between my ribs, a slight and constant pressure. Later, the poet Heid E. Erdrich introduces me to the concept of fetal microchimerism, the phenomenon of fetal cells being found in the mother decades after birth—"blood river once between you / went two ways / what makes us / own sole and sovereign selves / is only partially us," Erdrich writes in "Microchimerism"—and I wonder what alternate selves mothers carry in wombs that betrayed them, what muscle memories remain in the phantom space left behind when children have been delivered, when the wombs themselves are gone, or what we carry in wombs that, by choice or circumstance, never bear children. *Scientific American* tells me, "We all consider our bodies to be our own unique being, so the notion that we may harbor cells from other people in our bodies seems strange. Even stranger is the thought that, although we certainly consider our actions and decisions as originating in the activity of our own individual brains, cells from other individuals are living and functioning in that complex structure"—and I cup my palms together to imagine what my mother's three-pound cabbage-sized tumor would feel like, but the heft of my imagining disintegrates into the feel of my mother's hand in mine while the doctor attempts a second biopsy, necrotic tissue floating darkly in clear tubes, learning later that the cells simply fell apart when pathology tried to look at them. But I don't understand, not really. Are we our own unique beings or not? Science would suggest we are not. We exist within systems, networks, the matrix of family and friends, patterns. We are not alone. We are all connected, even on a cellular level, across time, space, and logic. Perhaps it is individuality that is the myth.

6

AGNES IS THE COLOR of fear, of orange cones and emergency vests, a color to startle, to wonder at the point where cancer has become the rule, not the exception. Every new diagnosis surprises me a little less. *It's cancer. It's always cancer.* It is fall in Minnesota and our days are getting shorter. I feel time as physical oppression. I am so angry in these days, my world a flare of bright orange. Anger is a secondary emotion, they say, a reaction to fear or vulnerability or frustration or injustice, an active reaction, rather than passive, and I walk the halls of the house, my belly simmering with something less than rage. The heft of cast iron in my hands feels right in a way my mother's light Club aluminum does not.

I am angry at the urgency they feel in giving my mother six months of destructive chemotherapy but not being worried when her blood counts are too low to receive treatment. For what feels like her oncologist forgetting she's a human being with a brain, with feelings, and this is something I will not ever forgive him for. We brush aside his poor bedside manner, as *that's just the way he is*, and my fingers tingle with resentment. For the subtext of *You have cancer and you're getting chemo—what do you expect?* For the nursing staff telling her, *again*, in voices that sound incredibly patronizing to my ear, *If your temperature gets to 100.4, you have two hours to get to the ER; make sure you wash your hands; make sure you avoid sick people—* or on her last visit, where her platelets were too low and her white blood cells were so scarce they could be individually counted, the nurse told her *to be extra careful with shaving—*and made motions with her hands like she was shaving her legs— and I could feel my brain seize. *Look around you, nobody here has hair, my mother also clearly has no hair, and you're telling her to be careful shaving her legs?*

My mother's friend A., recently diagnosed with lung cancer, sent an email where she reported with amused exasperation the frustrated and angry reaction of her son to not knowing more after her recent CT scan, and A. reminded him that she was pleased with the report, that she was—like my parents—*perfectly happy to accept things as they come. Oh,* my mother said to me when she read the email: *There are two of you!* My mother says she never felt patronized, or felt that she was treated poorly, but I felt it. Deeply. My father went so far this morning as to link such acceptance to maturity, *Not,* he hastily—but not hastily enough—added, *not that you're not mature.* At other times, he's suggested that perhaps I'm simply searching for somebody to be angry with. This might be true. I have the luxury of questioning these doctors when my parents do not. They need to trust that the oncologist knows exactly what he's doing, because if they cannot trust him, the consequences are unfathomable. My middle sister is a nurse: we are a family that trusts our medical professionals. We trust people who have risen to the tops of their fields to know what they are doing, whether they be cabinetmakers or world-class doctors. That is the way we function.

Maybe it's the job of children to bear emotion our mothers cannot voice. Maybe it's a role reversal none of us are ready for, when the children feel they must step in front of danger, into the path of those who would take advantage. I don't know where my distrust has come from—maybe the corporate takeover of education and medicine, the destruction of natural resources for the sake of profit, a political philosophy that calls business the savior of whatever ails you. We watch a pharmaceutical company jack the price of an AIDS drug or my nephew's EpiPen simply because they can. Maybe I feel more strongly the outrage of my mother being told to use Glad Press'n Seal wrap when she puts lidocaine on her port before she leaves home for treatments, rather than the medical-grade Tegaderm she was originally given. Our mothers, using kitchen wrap for medical purposes. Maybe, as a cook, I should appreciate the ingenuity, but I don't. I really don't.

7

THEY BROUGHT FOOD ON Tuesdays, because chemo happened on Mondays. Later, when my mother was regularly hospitalized for those 100.4 fevers, they rang the bell on Thursdays, too. The beeps and bells of the house were startling in such silence—the tri-beep of the thermometer a clear signal from down the hall that my mother was awake and checking for fever, the doorbell that set the dog to barking. Taking my mother to the emergency room became so commonplace in those days that we had a bag packed and ready near the door with her noise-canceling headphones, face masks and eye masks, her Kindle charging cords, and everything else she would need for an overnight stay. It was a mantra in those days—*you have two hours to get to the ER, no excuses*. The chemotherapy destroyed her white blood cells as well as her neutrophils, the baby white blood cells, and she was incredibly susceptible to infection. It was a terrifying way to begin treatment.

Our friends balanced hot lasagna, cold vegetables, yeasty bread that made bright steam in the dark winter air. They brought pork roast, beef roast, squash, potatoes. They rang the bell and offered their first vegetarian-cooking efforts, unnecessary apologies turning breath to laughter as they stood in the doorway. Nobody tells you how lonely cancer is, the fear of it hardening your skin into a shell as you watch your mother suffer with her bellyband after surgery, knowing that even when she can bend to tie her shoes, when she can take a shower without supervision, when she is permitted to lift her two small grandchildren, it will be less of an achievement and more a signal to proceed with the next terrible stage of treatment. When they talk about the cumulative effect of chemotherapy and radiation, they don't talk about the cumulative effect on the family: each stage takes longer for us to recover from, too.

In Greek, the practice of hospitality is called xenia, but more broadly it is the practice of showing kindness to strangers who appear on your doorstep and may or may not be gods in disguise. It is the hidden face, the unknowing, that is important: It does not matter who rings your doorbell. It could be anyone, or Anyone. For the Greeks, their religion now largely lost to myths of gods and Titans, xenia was about navigating a world where their gods did not live lives separate from them, a world where we find the divine in an ordinary salad of cucumbers, tomatoes, and onions on a Tuesday night, a moment where the individuality of cancer meets a community who will not let you walk this path alone. Maybe community is a myth, in the way that fetal microchimerism makes me wonder if individuality is a myth. Can it be Schrödinger's tumor, both and neither? Is that why we need myth, why we need metaphor, to cover the space of uncertainty? Why we need to consider the Greek practice of xenia, hospitality to the stranger who may or may not be the divine in disguise?

8

HERE IS WHAT IS not normal in this new world of cancer: I am not afraid. Not yet, at least. I am fully in determination-mode and my anger is not coming from a place of fear. My mother's oncologist at the Mayo Clinic says, "Disease wants to take tomorrow. Don't let it have today." But the truth is that we have not gone through cancer like this with anybody else in our family, which alters my perceptions, sends me to find color in carrots and cast iron because my fingers tingle with the need to do something. My maternal grandfather was diagnosed with leukemia in 1973, on his twenty-fifth wedding anniversary, when he bent to brush his teeth and hurt his back. I imagine that the conversations around cancer were much different in 1973. I remember the threat of losing my grandfather being a normal part of my growing up, but maybe because it was normal, we didn't have these conversations about cancer, about mortality. He died in his sleep in 2006. I've come to understand that my lack of fear right now is because my mother's doctors consistently refer to her as "cancer free," which gives us a false sense of security. I don't think about how unfair it is that my mother has cancer, because *she doesn't have cancer*—she's "cancer free" and the threat of losing my mother to cancer simply does not exist in these days—and then I realize how many of my innermost circle of friends have lost parents, how many of my classmates' parents passed away when we were in school. I will lose my parents eventually, this is obvious, but even now it is not something that penetrates my consciousness. My mother's uterus fully contained that tumor that brought us to this point and now it is gone, with all the cancer it contained. I don't know what fear looks like in this context. John Millington Synge wrote in *The Aran Islands* about fear: "The old man gave me his view of the use of fear. 'A man who is not afraid of the sea will soon be drowned,' he said, 'for he will be going out on a day he shouldn't. But we do be afraid of the sea, and we do only be drownded now and again.'"

9

MY MOTHER REMEMBERS MY grandmother storing fruits and vegetables in the basement fallout shelter, carefully wrapping each apple individually in tissue paper. In my childhood, my mother's garden was blanched and frozen and canned. To my sisters and me, Harvest—the Proper Noun—meant going out to the garden after we had gathered the last of the squash and beating the stinking, rotting vegetables to pulp with sticks and then hurling them into the distance as far as we could. Even now, even in adulthood, we still refer to Harvest only when our parents are out of earshot. My father hunted not only for enjoyment but for meat to fill the freezer. This time of year, the pause between harvest and winter, is one of preparation. My childhood was shelf stable because it had to be, not because my people lacked culinary imagination. Chicken, baked with white rice, condensed cream of chicken soup, and Lipton onion soup mix—warm and comforting and delicious and something my mother could put in the oven before church on a Sunday morning, and I wish I appreciated the crunchy rice around the edges of the pan in the way that I now deliberately make stuck-pot rice with my cast-iron skillet.

My grandmother was a skilled utilitarian cook who seemed to have never lost her fear of the Depression and the Dust Bowl, the rations of World War II, as she made the most out of the cheapest cuts of meat, preserved garden produce for the long winter, preparing and dreaming and fearing. Even now, fresh produce is not consistently available in the North Country, and yet, predatory grocery stores know that by the time January Thaw rolls around, we will pay premium prices for strawberries that aren't any good. On dark nights we made hotdishes with elbow macaroni, tomatoes we canned in August, and ground beef frozen when it was on sale. It would never have occurred to us to use fresh tomatoes to make a sauce for that hotdish, nor would it have occurred to make pasta from scratch. We would have considered it a waste of time and resources. As a culinary concept, we liked the idea of stability, of shelf-stable food. It suited our visions of ourselves as solid, grounded people who couldn't be blown about in the wind.

10

THE GREEKS BELIEVED THAT a woman's womb
could spontaneously start wandering in her body, causing
physical and mental problems. By the Renaissance, the wandering womb was considered the cause of more psychologi-
cal illnesses than physical ones. One solution developed over
time to keep the womb in place: a womb could not wander if
the woman was pregnant. Some considered that the problem
was that a woman's energy should be focused on her womb and
if she was not pregnant, that energy could escape to her brain.
My mother no longer has a womb. My sister is pregnant. My
youngest sister and I do not have children. My maternal grandmother bore one child; my paternal grandmother was mother
to five. My great-aunt K. never had children of her own, but
she wandered Central America with her own private pilot's license, then cycled through Europe in 1950 with a friend. My
father's aunt Edna never had children. The family story is that
her mother, Ida, had Edna sterilized in the 1920s under the
guise of an appendectomy because she thought Edna too frail
for children. I wonder if Edna ever knew the truth.

II

AGNES IS THE COLOR of risk, the risk of taking a chance on a thrift store skillet and entering a new world of wonder. I used to be afraid of cast iron, the idea that it is hard to use, hard to maintain, and *What's the point when Teflon exists?* We grew up with aluminum and that's what I knew: my grandmother's WearEver became mine when she moved into assisted living and my mother's Club is still in use after forty years. Cast iron—and Agnes—is nothing I know, but I find myself addicted. I think, *If I can't do it in the skillet, what's the point?* I learn how to bake cakes in the skillet, cobblers, pannekoeken, clafouti, eggs, hash, and the possibilities become delightfully endless. Building up the seasoning isn't hard when it's part of my routine: a wash, a dry, back on a warm burner to make sure the remaining water has evaporated, and then a thin swipe of oil. Agnes is now cured to the point of being indestructible and it's good to remember that. Agnes is a delicious constant in a world where nothing makes sense anymore.

There's a legacy to the cult of cast iron that I envy in these days of trying to understand cancer, a desire I have for specialized knowledge and not having to create a world from scratch, like someone has been down this road before, because the road less traveled is not always a path worth taking. I'm new to this cast iron world, my growing collection having come from thrift stores, colorful vintage Dutch ovens of varying colors and sizes, skillets like Agnes, but it is a world I want to understand, a community I want to be a part of. It's the equivalent of being passed down a hundred-year-old pan with seasoning like silk, the kind of long knowledge that rings with the voice of a great-grandmother you never met, the flavor of old laughter and bright pride.

12

ANOTHER ORIGIN STORY: I'M standing in my
friend A.'s bright kitchen in Ohio probably ten years ago
now, a 1950s white rental kitchen full of Le Creuset color
and a candy-pink KitchenAid mixer. I'm a little in awe, a
little intimidated, because A. knows what she's doing and
I know only enough to be dangerous. We teach together,
A., her husband, and I, and we live one street apart in this
small town. She's six inches shorter than I am, her husband
six inches taller. We're in our midtwenties with fairly fresh
master's degrees. A. is the friend who first brought me to
the Toledo Farmers' Market, the friend who once told me
I should open a bakery called Cakes and Shit Like That.
She's the one who taught me that cooking could be fun,
that it was not a betrayal of feminism, because who has time
for that nonsense when you're eating really good food?

A. is teaching me about cast iron and kale as we settle in for a girls' night. Her cast-iron skillet heats on the
stove, a pile of kale torn and piled on the counter next to
it. Greens are not something I know, beyond the fragile
leaf lettuce that my mother and grandmother would eat in a

bowl with sugar and milk. A. pours olive oil into the skillet and adds a pat of butter. I will learn later that this lowers the smoke point of the oil, but at this moment, I don't even know what a smoke point is. She piles the kale into the skillet, mounded beyond the sides of the pan, and starts to press it down with her tongs, then twists the seared greens. Press, twist, and toss, press, twist, and toss. When that entire mountain has wilted to a quarter of its size, she flicks salt and pepper into the pan, then finishes it with a squeeze of fresh lemon juice that sends up objection in steam. One more twist and she divides the pan between my plate and hers. We devour the kale in less time than it takes to prepare it. The butter and oil take down the bitterness, the bright of the lemon juice just enough to heighten the green flavor. It is this moment where I understand kale. Years later, I will swap kale for spinach in my favorite soups; I will add it to frittatas courtesy of Agnes as I teach my niece how to crack eggs. I will rarely have it fresh, but I always have a frozen bag or two waiting. I will sauté up fresh summer kale to eat with fried eggs, grateful that I don't have to share, but still wishing I could just hop one street over to exclaim *This is so good, you have to try this* anyway.

13

At Hackenmueller's Meats in Robbinsdale, the smell of smoking meat seeps through the brick walls into the street. The door to the butcher shop is old wood, the kind that makes you believe in your bones that the small shop has been in business for more than a hundred years. There's something here that rings of the 1960s, like the old photograph we have of my grandfather with his feet propped on his desk, horn-rimmed glasses on his nose. I imagine that man might have frequented a place like this, perhaps with my grandmother in a calf-length skirt holding my toddler mother by the hand. It is a satisfying image. The staff in their white aprons are energetic and knowledgeable enough that when I say, "I want bones for stock," they tell me I have choices. As a vegetarian in a butcher shop I trust their expertise, because until today, I didn't know the difference between stock and broth. I walk out with seventeen dollars' worth of soup bones and marrowbones. Bones are not cheap. Maybe they shouldn't be.

After we learned that embryonal rhabdomyosarcoma is a soft tissue cancer, one whose cells appear like the skeletal muscles of developing embryos, which is ironic considering the tumor developed inside her uterus, after the hysterectomy, after her first chemo treatment, after the failure of her antinausea medications under the doctor's terse orders *Don't let her throw up*, after several days passed before she could be convinced to eat anything, we wondered: *Starve a fever, feed a cold, but what do we do for cancer?* There is a desperation involved in feeding someone undergoing such treatments, not only because of the horror of it, not only because those chemicals change taste perceptions, but the failure to care for the most basic needs of someone you love so deeply is unacceptable. My mother's palliative doctor tells her that *dysgeusia* is the technical term for *food tastes like shit*, but this information does not help, so he prescribes Ritalin to stimulate her appetite. We laugh, knowing how many of her fourth grade students were also on Ritalin. We learn that our friend M. survived chemo on mashed potatoes and ice cream; F. couldn't tolerate sugar. My mother has trouble swallowing, complicated by a feeling she calls *dead belly*, like her entire midsection has filled with concrete, exacerbated by incessant belching, so my days are spent in her kitchen with the press of chicken under my fingers, the heft of beef bones, the slice and chop of carrots, onion, and celery, in pursuit of bone broth and a miracle.

14

THE YELLOW OF MY vintage four-quart Le Creuset Dutch oven named Estelle is the faded sunshine of summer lemonade, as viewed through a screen door from the distance of November. She is the first Dutch oven I found, the second of my cast iron collection, vintage Le Creuset like Agnes I could never afford in real life, sunny on a thrift store shelf for $4.99. I don't know why I felt like she needed a name or why I thought she had a Count Basie vibe, a blues personality with a sassy grin, the weight of her so spectacularly solid and comforting, but she was perfect to attempt bone broth for my mother at a point in my culinary experience where I knew nothing about such things. I hadn't made a soup from scratch, ever. The idea of a bone broth is to simmer a stock long enough—even up to twenty-four hours—to pull all the nutrients from the bones, the gelatin and collagen that can be drawn out only by time. Some consider bone broth the cure for everything and I was willing to try.

In these early days of chemotherapy where my mother's bones malfunction, where we come to terms with how many children are afflicted with this particular cancer, my elfin nephew shows me that his shoes light up when he runs, when he stomps, double-footed, around the kitchen to make them pulse. He is three years old. His shoes contain tiny blue orthotics the same color as the glasses he wears that turn dark in the sun. He has finally been diagnosed with a growth hormone deficiency that has kept him in the single-digit percentiles of growth and he begins daily injections he will need until he turns eighteen. The growth hormones will catch him up to his genetics, to help his bones grow to the height he was always destined to be. There will come a point where this is normal, that H. will not need both of his parents to hold him still while the plunger pierces his tiny leg, but we have not yet reached that stage. At some point, we expect that adult bodies will break down; there is something specifically awful about the malfunctioning of a child's body, which should be perfect in its newness.

The majority of research on my mother's cancer is on children, not adults. I have found only five studies of adults with embryonal rhabdomyosarcoma in the last thirty years, which estimate the number of adults with this cancer at four hundred, total. I look at my nephew, still small enough that I can perch him on the red stool on the kitchen counter so he can watch the earthmovers tear up the street in front of our house while my father takes my mother to chemo, and I just watch H. and wonder. The shots are working; he is growing. But he is still so small.

15

WE CONSIDER THE BETRAYAL of bone the worst
kind, a fracture of things we cannot fully accept. The week
before my middle sister moved to college, my father took
my sisters Rollerblading on the Heartland State Trail near
our home, the oldest Rails-to-Trails path in the state. He
fell and broke his hip. He was fifty years old, six foot five,
two hundred and twenty-five pounds: when he falls, something will give. In his parents' generation, the statistics of
death within a year of hip fractures are truly astounding.
We *work ourselves to the bone*, we *know things in our bones*, we consider the perfection of *bone structure*, and *sticks and stones may
break our bones*, but have we never lost the ancient philosoph-
ical idea that there are things we know intuitively, below
the level of consciousness? Is it that we attribute a certain
kind of knowing to our bones, a kind of discernment and
wisdom that cannot be gained otherwise, medieval ideas
of where wisdom and understanding are physically located
in the body? I know that the animals in the Ashfall Fossil
Beds in Nebraska are unique in that they were fossilized in
three dimensions. Most fossils collapse once the flesh has

decomposed, and if they collapse into a way that keeps the order of bones intact, we say that the skeleton is articulated, as if the order of bones allows us to speak of them. What is missing when we cannot articulate the bones, when they are telling us something other than what we expect them to say? What does it do to us when our bones betray us, when children do not grow, when mothers develop childhood cancers, when the bones we trust do not hold us? How do we articulate our lives, then?

16

THE STORIES OF CONSUMING the thing we want to become are ancient, old as folktales of Hansel and Gretel, the Christian Eucharist, warriors consuming defeated enemies. My pursuit of bone broth became the literal one-to-one equivalency of *If my mother eats bones, her bones will be strong*, because her chemotherapy makes her neutropenic, which means that without those white blood cells born in her bone marrow, she cannot fight infection. And yet, *consumption* is code for the scourge of tuberculosis. Consumption spun metaphors of weakness as virtue, as Susan Sontag famously questioned the war metaphors of cancer as ones of strength—"The bromides of the American cancer establishment, tirelessly hailing the imminent victory over cancer; the professional pessimism of a large number of cancer specialists, talking like battle-weary officers mired down in an interminable colonial war—these are twin distortions in this military rhetoric about cancer"—but in the first six weeks of my mother's chemotherapy, the food metaphors became my own reality: the *recipe* for her three-week regimens, the drug *cocktail* they pumped through her *port* every week. What is the purpose of metaphor except to understand what we absolutely cannot, to compare something we do not know to something we do? *It tastes like chicken*, after all. In those first six weeks, when my mother was hospitalized with those 100.4 fevers, she compared the bone pain of treatment to natural childbirth, something we could understand, even if we had not experienced it ourselves.

17

I REMEMBER THE FOOD shelf in the back of the hundred-year-old parish hall at the church, my father answering knocks on our parsonage door and giving food to whoever needed it. Looking back, even gatherings like Wednesday evening soup suppers during Lent—each one prepared by a different group in the church—were a way to make sure the larger community didn't go hungry in a rural world where church and school were the primary community gathering places. American relationships with food are often an expression of class and poverty and this is not new, from debates about free and reduced lunch for children to concerns about food deserts, both rural and urban. Politicians find it expedient to shame those who use SNAP to feed their children, stoking outrage over the idea that if one is poor, one does not deserve a birthday cake or fresh fruit. We are a food culture with a strong relationship between shame and food. This is the language we teach our children about who deserves food and who does not.

Perhaps we collectively tense around food because it has been vilified ever since we came out of the Depression, the Dust Bowl, the Second World War and had enough surplus that many of us did not worry about going hungry. The backlash against home cooking as a practice obviously coincided with convenience foods and women working outside the home, but it also seems to follow the rise of food as something to be feared and scorned. *Don't eat too much, you'll get fat; eat something, you're too skinny; fat is bad; salt is bad; sugar is bad.* My parents grew up in the age of the Clean Plate Club, the admonition to "think of all the starving children in China," which had become "all the starving children in Africa" by the time I was old enough. Food became a cultural tool of manipulation. Rather than teaching moderation, advertisements teach gluttony and austerity, practices that ring of immediacy, that advocate no planning for the future. *Eat all the meat you want, just no carbs!*

We trust the miracles of modern medicine to fix us when we have heart attacks, high cholesterol, and other health troubles that could be fixed by rethinking our relationships with food and the kitchen. Our health-care system is so broken that, where I grew up, benefit dinners were commonplace for families devastated by the costs of a car accident or a premature baby or by cancer. Maybe their insurance—if they had any—covers most of the cost, but insurance doesn't cover grocery money or the mortgage or lost wages. This is one reason we bring food for illness, the reason that the proceeds from the annual community

Fine Arts Concert benefit in my hometown went to support someone who couldn't support themselves. Where I teach, we have a food pantry because a significant number of our students are hungry. My parents' church funds Kid-Pack, which sends food home with elementary kids for the weekend; because so many are on free and reduced lunch, they know that those children will go hungry over the weekend until they come back to school. GoFundMe and other crowdsourcing fundraisers are certainly effective at reaching beyond the boundaries of a small town, making digital what we have done in person in my hometown for years with chicken suppers and spaghetti feeds, but it lacks the needed element of sharing a meal with your community as you gather in support and solidarity and knowing that you are not alone.

18

WHEN MY MOTHER WENT in for a wellness check in the summer, mildly concerned about discharge from a source she couldn't identify, her doctor told her to keep an eye on it. Wellness checks don't often include exams, so perhaps the error of her doctor not recognizing an issue, or of my mother not following up with her ob-gyn, is recognizable only in hindsight. But I wonder about those weeks when her belly was growing and her odd bleeding turned darker and heavier until it required a tampon, weeks where she hoped it was still nothing, as I expect that on some level, most women carry the genetic memory of our illnesses being diagnosed as hysteria. *It's probably nothing . . .*

When I was eighteen, seeking relief for the chronic debilitating headaches I'd been getting for as long as I could remember, the doctor told me *I don't believe you actually have migraines*. Something inside me froze at his words. My first solid memories of spiked pain date back to the age of three, pain on one side of my head that sent me to dark rooms, too-sensitive skin against the nubbly chenille of the bedspread in my maternal grandparents' guest room, yellow curtains pulled tightly against light. *I knew what I had.* My paternal grandmother also had them and it was one thing we had in common. So I kept a food diary for several months. I had a sensitivity to too much salt. I couldn't eat bell peppers. Artificial sweeteners were particularly bad. Flashing lights, whether strobes at a school dance or headlights of an oncoming car or fluorescent lights overhead, could trigger one. The doctor still didn't believe me.

I still remember the first time I heard one of my mother's cadre of medical professionals treat her like a hysterical cancer patient. It was the dark days of early December when she received her first chemotherapy, and we wanted to know what we needed to do to keep my mother's temperature down so we could keep her out of the hospital—and the care coordinator simply repeated, probably three or four times over the course of one phone call, that my mother *should wash her hands* and *stay away from sick people*. Nobody uses that voice on my father. I wanted to use my Teacher Voice—I don't have a Mom Voice for obvious reasons—a voice I have learned to use sparingly because it is cold and it is quiet and it is intense and when I use it on telemarketers, my mother raises her eyebrows in concern, and I wanted to snap at all those people: *She has cancer—and a master's degree—she's not an idiot.* I was angry at the patronizing ER doctor who sent my mother home with a 100.4 fever because *Why was she there with such a low fever?* He didn't say she was hysterical, or overreacting, but that's what I heard in his dismissal of her calmly trying to tell him, *again*, that she is a chemotherapy patient and she's supposed to come in for those kinds of fevers. When she came back to the ER the next day, because her fever had not gone away, he was a bit sheepish, having been reprimanded by her oncologist.

The truth is that we were lucky, even as we could not completely escape the historical habit of medicine to turn what women think or feel or worry about into commentary on who we are as human beings, that what we feel is the result of hysteria or our imagination. How many times have women heard a dismissive mocking of PMS when we express strong emotion? How often are we called *hysterical*? Even Denis Donoghue's 1978 *New York Times* review of Susan Sontag's *Illness as Metaphor* dismissed her work because she was angry. When we combine odd foods, how many times have we heard *Are you pregnant?* As the presidential election heated, how often did we hear the female candidate described as shrill, even as she worked through walking pneumonia and faltered in public, and not one woman I knew was surprised that she took no time to recover and was still lambasted for having no stamina? We listened to the gaslighting of America, being told that we hadn't just heard what we absolutely had just heard. *I don't believe you . . .*

19

THE WEATHER CHANNEL WARNS of a storm, but I knew in my right hip two days ago that it was coming. Studies have debunked the validity of those of us who know the weather in our bones, but the anecdotal evidence is compelling enough that I ignore the science and believe what I feel. *I don't believe you . . .* My ability to feel weather dates back to high school, to an afternoon of horseback riding with my best friend, who had horses. Was I fourteen? Fifteen? As we trotted down the dirt road near her house, the stirrup broke, spooking the horse, and I tried to hang on as the saddle slipped farther around his belly. The dread realization was that the terrified horse was not going to stop and I knew I could fall under his hooves, so I let go—just released my fingers and let go. I landed on my right side on the gravel road, my shoulder and my hip bearing the brunt, but I don't actually remember hitting the ground. My bones did not break, though I bear the scars more than twenty years later, the skin still pocked and rippled and just a shade pinker than the rest of my forearm, my knee. Where does knowledge live in our bodies, if not in our brains or our bones, memories written on our skin? It's the moment of letting go that I linger on these days, that moment between the decision and the hard ground, from holding tightly to releasing my fingers from their fist on the reins, the moment between lightning and the crack of thunder, the moment between the cause and the effect, that moment when a simmer turns into a boil, that moment of weightless gravity between what we think we should understand and what we do not and that moment where we grasp the air for anything solid and find nothing.

20

MY FAVORITE SOUS CHEF stands on a red stool so she can crack eggs for me, a task she has recently mastered. Her blond hair escapes its ponytail as she bends her head in concentration and carefully taps the egg on the counter, tucking her little thumbs into the break and prying the shell apart, deliberate in her attention to keep shells out of the bowl. She looks at my skillet named Agnes on medium heat on the stove and says reverently, "Aunt Kinny, I *love* that pan." The finely sliced onions sizzle gently. The orange of the pan glows with cheer, the black of the cast-iron surface gleams like satisfaction.

I have been informed that the gender-neutral term for niece/nephew is *nibling*. I find this delightful, the sounds of it rolling on my tongue. *I'm cooking with the niblings today.* It even sounds delicious. I like that C., in her toddler-inability to pronounce my name, named me *Kinny*. Her father's sister became *YoYo*. I find the label for women like me, PANK—Professional Aunt, No Kids—mildly amusing. It is the lack, the absence, that is strange, abnormal, the way we cannot conceive of other modes of creating and maintaining family. C. and H.—and whoever their new sibling will be—have only aunts and I like the language of it.

I learned how to aunt by watching it done well. We often describe my father's aunt K. as the most right-brained person we've ever met, whose creative talents never led to culinary success as we often joke that K. could burn water. A couple of weeks ago, she sent my father an email that ended with "Gotta go change clothes. Going dancing tonight" and nobody was sure if she was kidding or not. She has neuropathy in her legs and can't feel them, but it's entirely within her character to go dancing anyway. She was always delighted to see us when we visited her in California, truly delighted, and we recognized that as rare. About the time I was sixteen or seventeen, I became her protégé as the apprentice family historian, which connected us even more strongly. H. was born on K.'s ninetieth birthday. What we do not know is that my sister's third child will be born on the day K. passes away.

I also learned how to aunt from my father's sister, T., who is twelve years younger than my father, the youngest of the five siblings. My earliest memories of her involve being in my grandparents' house and running into her room in the dark of the morning and jumping on her bed in much the same way C. does with me now. I couldn't have been more than three or four, but I remember the curtains pulled against the morning and I remember the red of Tab cans. Aunt T. and Uncle R. were always glad to see us and it was never the perfunctory hug that adults often give kids. Our visits became joy-filled spaces of Mongolian BBQ, griddles set up in their backyard, tables mounded with anything you could think to put in them. It was from them I learned the delight of sesame oil, something absent from my Scandinavian culinary world. T. and R. wanted to be with us, not just around us, and I remember how that made me feel as a kid. It's not an easy role to play, not if one wants to live up to their example.

Aunting is an active verb, the extension of creating a family. My youngest sister and I work to create the relationship on our own terms: my sister, also a PANK, works for the state government and makes civic engagement as natural to the kids as breathing. It's never too young to march and protest. My sisters took C., at the age of four months, to walk her first picket line to support her mother's fellow nurses on strike for better patient safety and quality of care. When my niece was eight months old, my youngest sister took her when she went to vote. My nephew, at four months, joined his family on the lawn of the Minnesota State Capitol for the signing of the marriage equality bill. Today C. cracks eggs for me and we bake a cake.

21

THE IDEA OF CANCER seemed so large that we needed to find any way to reduce it to what we could comprehend. Lia Purpura, in her essay "On Miniatures," writes, "Miniatures offer changes of scale by which we measure ourselves anew. . . . You are large enough to hold such things fully in hand. You obtain all the space around it." She adds, "Whether we are, in relation to them, omniscient or companionably small beings, miniatures invite us to leave our known selves and perspectives behind." When my niece was born, I wanted her to stay tiny forever. At five pounds, seven ounces, C. was too delicate for newborn clothes and her days in the special care unit—having missed the cutoff by one ounce—gave us time to find preemie clothes that fit while she figured out how to maintain her blood sugar and keep her weight up. Three years later, when my nephew was born weighing four pounds, nine ounces and released from the NICU after two weeks, we took pictures of him dressed in the Cabbage Patch clothes our mother had made for our dolls when we were children.

When they were each six months old, the niblings

traded clothes with Paddington Bear, much the same way my mother had done with me at that age: in the faded photograph, I am wearing Paddington's blue jacket, yellow hat, and yellow plastic boots, and he is wearing my pink overalls. C. and H. have joined the tradition and we laugh at how silly it is that the children wear doll clothes. We sober at the reminder that H. did not grow at all between the ages of six and nine months, diagnosis finally coming that he was allergic to dairy and eggs, and I worry about the child my sister is carrying right now, what kind of complications might be in store. There is so much worry in my blood these days. With my bright, cheerful nephew, stuck in fraction-digits of growth percentiles, my wish for smallness seemed to come true as he literally stayed tiny for longer than he should have.

22

WHEN *PUMPKIN* BECAME A term of endearment is a matter of debate, offset from *sweetness*, from *sugar*, *sugarplum*, *honey*, even the saltiness of *peanut*, the food names we call each other, the tasty and the sweet, the foods that give us the most visceral pleasure, the greatest joy, the fullest sensory experience. My littlest *pumpkin*, my littlest *peanut*, my nephew H., is three. After his allergy diagnosis, my mother took to the social media trend of painting one of her Halloween pumpkins teal to signify a peanut-free space with nonfood treats for other kids who have allergies. Once, I made an offhand comment to H. about driving his mother nuts and H. immediately started crying.

What? I asked, alarmed.

Don't say nuts, he whispered, curling up into a ball on the couch.

Nuts? Why not?

I'm allergic to nuts, he said so quietly I had to strain to hear him and I took a moment to marvel at the idea that he thought the word itself could hurt him.

H. was a giraffe for Halloween this year, his costume

punctuated by round blue glasses, trailed by my sister's black Lab, Marley, dressed as a lion, embarrassed as only a big dog can be.

When the niblings walk through the door with a basket of miniature pumpkins and squashes not designed for eating, we exclaim, *Oh, pumpkins from our pumpkins!* On my stove sits Penelope Pumpkin, the third addition to my cast iron collection, a two-quart Le Creuset cocotte, pumpkin shaped and pumpkin colored, small and bright and ridiculous. I have no explanation for why the pots were named, from Agnes to Estelle to Minnie to Penelope, but perhaps the silly naming counteracted so much unknowing around me.

Is it too much to say that *I love this pot*, the kind of visceral happiness that should be reserved for people, not inanimate objects? And yet: *I love this pot*. We tend to disparage the pleasure of *things*, the joy we gain from objects, but in their best sense, *things* are icons. In the tradition of religious iconography of Orthodox Christianity, icons are windows between ourselves and God, the invisible webs of connection we need when the world tilts sideways. Sometimes the link is between people who have gone, but the *thing* still exists. Maybe it collects dust on a shelf, the *thing* too fragile and precious to be a part of everyday life, but it is still an icon to that person, that memory, that feeling. When I brought home Penelope Pumpkin, I admitted that my thrifted stockpile of vintage cast iron in shades of Descoware and Le

Creuset and Cousances might have gotten out of control, but the collection of them in what I would come to call the Cook Nook brings me shimmering joy. In the case of Penelope Pumpkin, I'd long wanted something small and beautiful that could live on the back burner and make small quantities of soup for one person. So I set Penelope there, cheerful in that classic color they call "flame," comical in her scalloped shape and offset handle, something joyfully satisfying in her smallness.

Around Halloween, we are directed to introduce small amounts of dairy into H.'s diet. My mother does not like cheese and she never has. H. will eat an entire box of macaroni and cheese by himself, which is amazing for such a tiny creature. Later, I will experiment with *cacio e pepe* and fettuccine Alfredo, the emulsified pastas of cheese and pasta water that come together like magic without cream. Not long ago, my mother told me she does not like the way cheese squeaks against her teeth; she can tolerate cheese if it is part of a recipe, and I return to my childhood memories of bright orange cheese, the Colby and the cheddar and the Velveeta, which ring for me now in the same pumpkin orange as Penelope, who makes Parmesan broth against the chill of fall. Before long, the house takes on the most spectacular scent, a rich kind of sharpness, what the most potent love must taste like in those moments where we are most helpless, deep in sleep or fear. *Eating our feelings* is pejorative, something shameful in this desire to find comfort in food, but I find delight in the fat from the melting cheese having woven itself into lacelike bubbles on the surface, slightly darker than the golden broth, and *eating my feelings* seems healthy and desirable, the movement back into murmurs of *pumpkin* and *honey* as my small nephew fights against sleep in my arms.

23

WHAT I'VE LEARNED ABOUT making Parmesan broth is simply this: however you make it, just do. I started with Smitten Kitchen's recipe, half a pound of Parmesan rinds in two quarts of water, but what I learned was that you should always use cheesecloth, because otherwise, it's like chipping concrete off the pot. I would learn that the fat in Parmesan cheese is water soluble, which makes broth possible. Later, I would abandon the cast iron altogether and employ the slow cooker for greater quantities without more effort. Parmesan broth was a moment of moving from knowing nothing into knowing something, a precious shift in how I was learning this new way to navigate the kitchen and the world of cancer. How much I learned in those first few attempts at Parmesan broth, how to create a new language of this type of food, how to translate this new understanding from one table to the next, because my mother's doctors are still talking to us in food metaphors. My youngest sister researches the after-visit reports sent home with my mother, trying to translate the language, but making no headway because all the research on embryonal rhabdomyosarcoma is on children. Research was useless and the unknowing gnawed at us, so I reread Susan Sontag's *Illness as Metaphor* alongside my cookbooks. Sontag writes, "My point is that illness is *not* a metaphor, and that the most truthful way of regarding illness—and the healthiest way of being ill—is one most purified of, most resistant to, metaphoric thinking. Yet it is hardly possible to take up one's residence in the kingdom of the ill unprejudiced by the lurid metaphors with which it has been landscaped" and I almost smile at the lurid colors of the cookware around me, the landscaping of this house quieted so my mother can heal, the clarity of Parmesan broth on the stove. I will keep my metaphors awhile longer.

24

On its face, the idea of a broccoli cobbler is suspicious, the way that I use Agnes to cook the celery and onion until translucent, add flour, cook for a few minutes until the raw flour taste has disappeared, then stir in the broth and milk and let the mixture thicken, adding broccoli and seasonings as the mixture becomes less soup-like and more hotdish-like. The original recipe calls for cans of cream of broccoli soup, but it's just as easy to make it from scratch and I can control the sodium more easily. I haven't bought canned soup in years. The oven heats to 400 while I make biscuits and spoon them directly onto the broccoli mixture. Because the cast-iron skillet is transferrable from stovetop to oven, it's simple enough. The blobs of biscuit dough turn into golden cobbles across the bubbling broccoli and even the most skeptical find that if I don't actually call it broccoli cobbler, they'll eat it with great enthusiasm. Language matters.

While the idea of broccoli cobbler might be suspicious, it is not actually absurd: the idea of the absurd, to philosophers, is about the fundamental disharmony in the world and the human response to it. Religion, science, yoga, art are modes of seeking understanding in the world in the same way, as each offers its own answer to that disharmony. Even cooking, as I see it, is its own philosophy, each way of thinking based in a desire to find meaning between breaths, in the space between bubbles bursting on the surface of a rolling boil. The absurd lives in the conflict between the human desire to find value and meaning in life and the events of a life and the human inability to do so. Because there is so much knowledge in the universe, fully under-standing something is not possible. In these days, I like the idea of it, the way I roll it in my hands, press my fingers into it like dough.

Johannes de Silentio believes that absurdity is not "logically impossible" but "humanly impossible." Philos-ophers like Søren Kierkegaard and Albert Camus, among others, considered that there are only three responses to this in-between space: The first is suicide, which philos-ophers dismiss as absurd in itself. The second is developing a religious or spiritual belief system that allows for open spaces ("leaps of faith"), but most philosophers also dis-card this option as unviable. The third is the acceptance of the absurd, which involves acknowledging the absurd and living your life in spite of your inability to come to any sort of meaning. On its face, then, my collection of thrifted Le Creuset and Descoware and Cousances and Copco is not absurd, the Cook Nook stacked with dark brown sugar and Nordic Ware cakelet pans in the shape of bugs, the cobalt corkboard in the style of Julia Child hung with bright vintage color, the skillets, the Bundt pans that I know by name. It is, perhaps, ridiculous, but it is not absurd.

25

MY MOTHER WANTS COMFORT food in the days after chemo: she wants Malt-O-Meal or she wants eggs and
toast and we bring it to her bedroom on a hammered aluminum tray her parents received as a wedding gift in 1948.
I try to talk her into a mug of chicken stock or steel-cut
oats to encourage her toward any consumption of nutrients
beyond the simple beige carbohydrates she craves, but she
wants what she wants and I cannot blame her for that. I will
feed her whatever she feels she can eat. She has never been
sick before, and as a result, my mother has always seemed
indestructible, even in her five-foot-three way of making
sure all our worlds spun in the right direction at the right
speed. She was always the comfort for us. But it was in those
moments after her surgery and she did not understand the
pain scale and she breathlessly described her pain as 3 when
it was closer to 9 or 10, and she made little moaning sounds
that didn't have enough air pressure or volume to be moans
at all, when her resemblance to her own mother was incredibly acute, the way she scrunched her eyes against a body
that could not tell the difference between good trauma and

bad trauma—it knew only that it had been cut open—and I held her hand, soft, swollen from surgery fluids, and the wrinkles on the back of her hand were indistinguishable from my grandmother's. Comfort is not something one can do for oneself. Comfort is external.

Comfort is a full-body experience, the emotional need being taken care of through the physical. *Hygge* has become a popular, elusive aspiration. It's our fingers in the dog's fur, our hands holding our mother's as she lay in her bed after the hysterectomy, the first major surgery of her sixty-five-year life. Comfort has the quality of warmth to it, a fire, a hug, a blanket. It is our mother, trying to warm under her electric throw, shivering because her chemo makes her cold. We find we do not need comfort food as much in the summer, the external need for warmth coming from triple-digit heat indices. I wonder about what we crave when our world is just a little off-center, my theory resting on preferences for simple carbohydrates and salt, food that is warm and easily chewable. Some research suggests it may be the body's response to exhaustion simply because those carbohydrates are more easily digestible. A poll among friends bears this out: macaroni and cheese, grilled cheese and to-mato soup, mashed potatoes, tuna or chicken or tater tot hotdish. Mine is a fried-egg sandwich.

Minnesota hotdish is ingrained in us as comfort food, memories of what we, in our family, came to call Walter

Mondale Hotdish, the classic combination of elbow macaroni, ground beef, and tomatoes, as my father came home one day, wondered what was for dinner, and asked, as Walter Mondale had once done, *Where's the beef?* When Al Franken was first elected to the US Senate in 2011—after a recounted and contentious election, which bookended his contentious departure from the Senate—he hosted the first annual Minnesota Congressional Delegation Hotdish-Off, and each year since, the newspapers report that *a good time was had by all*. That first year, Amy Klobuchar won with her Taconite Tater Tot Hotdish. Representative Tim Walz is a three-time winner. With Franken's departure, his replacement, Tina Smith, has taken over the hosting duties. The Hotdish-Off has become a tradition, with the winners—and everyone's recipes—duly reported in the *Star Tribune* in the same way I remember the social reports in my own small-hometown paper where *Mrs. S., Mrs. O., and Mrs. L. gathered at the home of Mrs. K., where the hostess served coffee and apple crisp, and a good time was had by all*.

There's a beautiful stability to the formula of a hotdish, the starch, the protein, the binder, the crunch on top, the way flavors move into the warmth of the air, the way it can be reheated many times without losing its quality. It's easy to glamorize the food of my northern Minnesota childhood as being something more exciting than it was, the need we had for the garden's produce in the winter, but there was satisfaction in it. Hotdish is practical food, easy to freeze for when it's needed, what you bring for the arrival of a new baby or illnesses like cancer when you know the family does not have enough time or energy to eat more than cereal from the box. The science of comfort food breaks down into the emotional comfort provided by foods that we associate with good memories—the areas of the brain that are activated when we crave certain foods are those that most clearly link memory and pleasure—but comfort food can also represent the body's deficiency in nutrients it needs to function.

But when we think of the chemicals required for comfort, for happiness, even though consuming carbohydrates and sugars can spark serotonin levels in our brains, it is the acceptance of that particular gift that releases dopamine, the chemical released when we achieve a goal. Our bodies are curious creatures, the way we can be surrounded by the tenor-note scent of Parmesan broth in the air and crave the salt of it, or the insistent need for sweet to fill a space inside us we would like to ignore. Can it all be reduced to chemicals, the presence or lack of them, the chemotherapy that is the reason we are here in the first place, the chemical combination of hydrogen and oxygen to create the snow pattering on the windows as I preheat the oven, choose a recipe, and wrap myself in a blanket in front of the fire while it cooks?

26

THE SECOND RECIPE IN the dark blue 1949 Faith Lutheran Church cookbook from Forest Lake, Minnesota, is my great-grandmother Florence's recipe for Scalded Rye Bread. Rye bread is common to the Swedes, this hardy grain that could survive both Sweden's and Minnesota's soils and climates. The recipe is sparse on details, filled with assumptions Florence made about the women who would read this recipe. They might not have known why they scalded the milk, but the science would come clear in later decades that it alters the proteins in the milk and creates a better bread. It doesn't have anything to do with pasteurizing milk, I learned. I tried the recipe, but even with the help of Google, I couldn't decipher it. That batch ended up in the trash. I found another recipe, this time for Swedish limpa, the sweet rye bread flavored with anise. I'm fond of the stronger-flavored ryes, the dark ones, the marbled ones, but limpa is a special favorite, even though it's not part of my family's historical repertoire. This recipe comes from the internet and I smile at the number of recipes in my mother's and grandmother's recipe boxes that were clipped from newspapers and magazines. Perhaps there is nothing new under the sun.

What I've learned is that the anise dissolves into the bread after a day or so, making it well worth the wait to cut into the loaf, but I rarely have the self-control. My stomach muscles clench, tighten, as if I haven't eaten in days. There's so much I want to know, to understand about what is happening to my mother, why it has to happen to my mother, and the lack feels visceral. Can we consume knowing? Can we waste away without it? I feel desperate, wild with hunger. I wish I knew more about how to judge the development of gluten, about which breads I should use the windowpane test on. I'd like to know more about how structures of strength develop, how the complex matrix holds things together so that the gas produced by the yeast can expand without everything collapsing. In these days where I can't voice my frustration with this world I don't understand, there is nothing more satisfying than the punch to the middle of the risen dough and watching it deflate, the inexplicable wonder of knocking a loaf on the bottom and listening for the hollow sound, the beautiful, perfect sound of nothingness.

27

WHEN I WAS YOUNG, my mother made bread weekly.
I remember the honey whole wheat dough rising in the
yellow Tupperware bowl on top of the fridge, a conve-
nient place, the warm rise of yeast in those hours of three-
children-under-the-age-of-five. In the early 1980s in
a town of a hundred people, it was easier and probably
cheaper for my mother to make bread than it was to buy
it at the grocery store. When I set out to attempt bread in
these days, it seems more complicated than simply trying a
new recipe. It can't be that I want to exercise the privilege
of returning to a time when the generations of women in
my family either by accessibility or finances needed to make
bread if they wanted it—and to be without bread was to have
a house without a roof. My mother made bread. My grandmothers did not, because they did not have to. I imagine
that my maternal great-grandmother, Florence, made a
dozen loaves a day during threshing season, a dozen pies
in addition to meat and potatoes, when womanhood and
reputation were thoroughly judged by how well a farmwife
fed those threshers. Your worth not just as a person but as

a woman was judged by the work of your hands. Failure was not an option. If you did not feed the threshers well, they did not return.

My father's mother and her sister were in their forties during the height of second-wave feminism, where kitchen failures were badges of honor. They were each working, my grandmother as a nurse, my great-aunt as the first female draftsman hired by Ryan Aeronautical. A thousand miles away from them, I grew up with such mentalities—it was desirable to be a bad cook, to burn food, to be utterly hopeless in the kitchen—even though such ideas were not a part of my mother and grandmother's philosophy. Sometimes I try to understand the difference, between Minnesota and San Diego, between short growing seasons and produce available all year, differences in education among the women in my family, but I have not found a suitable pattern. My mother, also highly educated, raising children in rural Minnesota in the 1980s, could not afford to be a bad cook. To be a bad cook was to waste food and that waste was unacceptable.

28

MY FATHER'S FAMILY HAS a history of figs, a family food history of southern California fruit, the pears, persimmons, and fig trees common enough to their backyards in the way that pines were to my childhood. The classic Babine Family Recipe for pickled figs comes down through my father's grandmother, Kayo, and her sister, Edna, who were born in Deadwood, South Dakota, and moved with their mother to San Diego after the death of their father in 1906, when the doctors told Ida that she would not survive another winter in Deadwood. What happened, though, is that Ida dumped her girls in a convent school and rarely visited. It's hard for me not to judge Ida's mothering, but the truth is I don't know what drove her choices. She had, after all, buried her daughter's twin sister as well as her husband by the age of thirty.

"Pickled figs" is a misnomer of sorts, because they are not exactly pickled, but candying them in this way echoes the preserving of food so inherent to my mother's Minnesota heritage, both the Germans and the Swedes. Five pounds of figs equals three quarts. Boil two quarts of water and a half cup of baking soda, then pour over the figs and let stand for five minutes. Pour off the soda water and rinse the figs with hot water. On the first day, make the syrup: one cup of water, twelve cloves, six cinnamon sticks, six cups of sugar, and one cup of apple cider vinegar. Pour the boiled syrup over the drained figs. Boil ten minutes for three days. On the third day, drain the juice and boil down to a thick syrup. Pour over the figs and can in clean jars. Be sure the syrup covers the figs. The flavor of clove and fig is too strong for me to enjoy eating them with my fingers out of the jar, like my father does. I do wonder, however, how those figs, that syrup would be in a cake, perhaps a ripple running through a rich, buttery pound cake.

I wonder how we can take this generational memory that tastes of San Diego, of memories of my grandmother Marion's beloved fig tree, and change the angle of the flavors, just a bit, simply because figs are not a part of my own historical food. The story of figs is worth telling, in shades of 1950s black-and-white photography, capturing a moment in time and one simple truth: my grandmother loved her fig tree, loved it fiercely. In those deckle-edged days, my mischievous grandfather told my father and his brothers that the way to get the best figs, the biggest figs, was to pinch off the little ones and throw them over the fence. Dutifully, my father and his three younger brothers followed his lead, because they knew how much their mother loved her fig tree. Throughout that summer, my grand-mother could not understand why her tree was not pro-ducing. Then came the day when they were caught and I can imagine four dark-headed boys, tall for their age, lined up in front of their mother to account for what they'd done, the crime not the waste of food but the violation of the tree itself, destroying something that was not theirs to destroy. Someday, on the back of the recipe card for pickled figs that bears her handwriting, I will write this story in the tone of her voice.

29

A SLICKLY OILED BEEF roast waits on the counter in the days approaching the winter solstice while my three-quart oval flame Descoware Dutch oven named Minnie heats hot enough to sear. The danger to cast iron is in rapid heat changes, so I start the pan on medium, then gradually turn it higher as it warms. My favorite Food Network chef, Alton Brown, taught me that you should always oil the meat, not the pan, because the oil will smoke before it's hot enough to sear. My mother has requested pot roast, the first time in a long time she has requested anything specific to eat. Sometimes I braise the roast with leftover red wine, sometimes with broth, sometimes with water, sometimes with a generous dusting of my favorite spice blends. Into a low oven for a few hours, and I add the carrots and potatoes partway through the cooking. It is December, my mother is three weeks into chemotherapy, and I am still learning what it means to be a vegetarian cooking for carnivores.

While living in Ohio, I moved to ethical sources of meat. In 2012, while living in Nebraska, I could no longer justify the water used to grow corn in places not meant to be farmed to feed cows who were not designed to eat corn, because the Great Plains is pumping out the Ogallala Aquifer at five times its replenishment rate. I stopped eating almonds, except as part of our Christmas rice pudding tradition, because each almond is equivalent to one gallon of water in drought-ravaged California. I come from a place they call Lakes Country in north-central Minnesota and I might argue that water, not blood, runs in my veins. There are ninety lakes in a ten-mile radius around my hometown and my mother always wondered how she could raise three kids in northern Minnesota who didn't like fish. Water is my drink of choice, bubbly if I can get it. I object to factory farming on ethical grounds, but beyond that, I object to the water pollution those farms create. Some statistics indicate 40–50 percent of Minnesota's water is polluted, most of it the result of runoff from farms. Because my vegetarianism does not rise out of animal rights issues, not only do I not have a problem with meat, I've missed cooking it.

And yet, I am not a purist and I am not always consistent: I can't be, coming from this place where we must have food brought to us in the months we cannot grow it ourselves. My childhood home had two giant freezers in the basement. When I got my first good job, the first major purchase I made was a 2.4-cubic-foot chest freezer. When butter goes on sale at the grocery store, I stock up and toss it in the freezer. The last time this happened, I ended up with twenty-five pounds, which is usually enough to last until the next time it goes on sale. My brand of vegetarian ethics means I don't get too wrapped up in the ethics of Jell-O, marshmallows, or rennet in cheese, but the carnivore's spatula does not stir the vegetarian dinner. Picking pepperoni off a pizza does not make it into something I will eat. I like my SodaStream because it cuts down on waste, but I struggle with the ethical issues of the company's West Bank factory, and I try to justify it by remembering that I bought mine at a thrift store, which doesn't actually solve my ethical conundrum. My food ethics knows I should form my shopping habits around immigrant rights and labor, that I should find the line between the farmers I grew up with and the environmental impact of center-pivot irrigation systems that are pumping the aquifers dry, because I know what happens when ethics collapse. I know what happens when a Texas billionaire has enough power to convince the USGS to redraw the map of the Ogallala Aquifer so he can build a for-profit toxic waste dump on top of the major source of water in the Great Plains. Without irrigation, the farmers in my hometown run a much greater risk of crop failure. But last year, for the first time, the spring that feeds the Crow Wing chain of lakes was dry.

30

MY SISTERS HAVE EACH been vegetarian for more than a decade. My small niece claims to be vegetarian when she does not want to eat what is in front of her, like the corn casserole we served for Thanksgiving once. She was not pleased when we laughed and told her it was vegetarian. My nephew, with his dietary allergies, ate almost nothing beyond bananas and Costco avocados and turkey as his parents attempted to manage his nutrition. H. wasn't a picky eater; it was a matter of making sure whatever he ate had enough fat and nutrients to balance his dairy and egg allergies, which led to his favorite 'cados in the winter. He transitioned from breast milk to hypoallergenic formula to rice milk; to the latter they added olive oil to add more fat into his diet. We learned that putting babies on soy milk too early can lead to soy allergies. Our parents and my brother-in-law retain their carnivorous ways. We make it work. This is our food history, the one we are continuing to write. Cooking, for me, is a mode of self-sufficiency that is also about fitting into a network of a family and a place.

These days, I find myself reverting to the old ways of

cooking, of my mother's pot roast and boiled potatoes and hotdish, searching through my recipe boxes and cookbooks and the internet for anything she will eat. Comfort food is part of it, meat and potatoes that remind my mother of good things, lemon chicken made with canned cream of broccoli soup that I remember cooked in her electric fry pan on the counter that I would attempt to make from scratch with the help of Agnes. I might know that potatoes with dairy equals a complete protein, but mashed potatoes was just one of the few things she could and would eat when her chemo caused the *dead belly* feeling in her stomach or when she developed mouth sores and the only thing I could think to feed her was broth I would never taste made from the chicken I had roasted in my yellow pot named Estelle.

31

I DREAM OF KITCHENS in muted matte wall colors, saturated slate blue and sage green and goldenrod, of kitchens facing east to catch morning, a place to trace the change of one moment into another across a checkered black-and-white tile floor I've wanted since the first time I played Clue as a child. I dream in the quiet of morning dark, of being the only one stirring the air currents in this space because I choose to live a solo life, finding the line between my individual personality and the community around me. I dream of a bright teakettle on the stove rattling the morning into existence, though the reality is a red electric kettle on the counter. In this particular incarnation of my dream, the doorway from the adjacent dining room into the library is a hidden passageway, perhaps simply a bookcase on a quiet hinge, opened only if you know the secret book that hides the latch. Dreaming of houses I do not own, of kitchens that are not yet mine, is a way of taking control in a world where I have none. I fixate on things that I know are absurd, because these become known quantities. I could, if prompted, provide a full tour of these imaginary cupboards.

I dream of old cabinets refreshed in white paint, thrifted dressers turned into kitchen islands, perhaps with stools where visiting nieces and nephews decorate Christmas cookies in the warm and vanilla of a cold December afternoon, cocoa mustaches and sticky marshmallow fingerprints, where my niece holds a spoonful of bright sprinkles for spritz in one hand and tells her grandfather, "Boppa, you're not very good at this, but you're a little bit good at this," and my nephew simply, wordlessly, happily dumps an entire bottle of green sprinkles on a single cookie. I dream of where to put my vertical pot stand full of vintage color, the easy access of my cast iron collection, with one of them simmering a perfect winter soup on the stove, the color and scent vibrant with the sharpness of Parmesan broth against the neutral of the cabinets and appliances and the exclamation of someone walking into the house and *Oh, that smells wonderful!* I am protective of my space, but I like to fill it with people I love.

But I stand in my mother's golden medium-oak kitchen, dreaming and fearing the long months ahead, the chemo, the CT scans, neighbors bringing food, neuropathy and chemo brain, needing to indulge the fantasy of everything being as it should be if we were to design everything perfectly, down to its last detail, a world where we can control something, anything, a world where we do not worry about *cancer*, a world where we are not caught unprepared, a world where we dream in color.

In other angles of light, I dream of setting my future table with other thrifted treasures, my yellow-and-blue linen tablecloth that still bore its forty-nine-cent price tag when I found it, perhaps a brunch table waiting for banana bread or rhubarb Bundt cake. Perhaps I have hung pegboard painted in the same color as the walls to hold my growing collection of intricate Nordic Ware Bundt pans, the practical becoming decoration. Perhaps the table is set with my eclectic teacup collection, most of which came from my father's grandmother who collected them on her travels. My love for thrifting is not just the expression of a frugal nature, influenced by maternal grandparents who grew up during the Depression and the scarcity of World War II rations, the admonition to *buy things once and buy them right*, but it's also about creating my own world of wonder, seeking this joy of discovery, an acquisition of *things* I think I should have at this point in my life. It's about creating a history that I can walk into, one I don't have to think about my place in. Certainly there are generational aspects to our relationship to *things*, the trappings of domestic life that have changed from our parents' or grandparents' generations, the *things* that signaled that one was a fully functioning adult member of society and many of which have been rejected by Millennials and Generation X. Very few of my friends registered for china and stemware when they married. When my youngest sister bought her house several

years ago, I commented that it felt like a grandparents'
house. My sister looked at me, visibly swallowing her initial
reaction, and calmly asked, *What do you mean by that?* I had to
explain that it felt lived in, that it felt comfortable, that it
felt like it had a long history of stories and the boss coming
for Sunday dinner. She nodded in agreement.

I dream of the chaos that will descend as niblings,
present and future, burst through my front door. I dream
of handing my cancer-free mother a mimosa of sparkling
wine and tangerine sorbet in turquoise Fostoria Rhapsody
stemware and telling her to make herself comfortable, that
I have the kitchen under control, but this will not be true
since the kitchen is the place to gather, and it will be full
of my sisters, perhaps little ones underfoot. Perhaps I have
made a frittata in my beloved Agnes with summer tomatoes
that I roasted with olive oil and froze for the winter, to be
served on toasted rye bread I made from my great-grandmother's recipe in my cast-iron Dutch oven. The table
might be set with my gleaming white Noritake Derry china,
which I bought myself when I was in my midthirties because
I wanted china and I wasn't going to wait for my mother to
die to inherit hers. Maybe I ask the niblings which crystal stemware we should use, Marion's or Phyllis's wedding
stemware, or the pretty glass set my grandmother Marion
acquired with Blue Chip Stamps, because even though the
crystal is fragile, it's still supposed to be used, not catch

dust. Maybe I will ask them which color of napkins they prefer. I like the precision of a tablescape, how the colors I have chosen might create cheer or relaxation or excitement in those who sit at my table and eat my food. My mother taught us, as her mother taught her, that you should always set your table first, so if your guests arrive and the food is not ready, you look like you have anticipated their arrival.

32

THE SECRET TO CHICKEN soup is to start with a
chicken, a whole one, three to four pounds. Chicken soup
is a pot of deliberate attention, a thing that contains everything that you and the chicken have to give, so if you have a
yellow Le Creuset that you have named Estelle for no good
reason other than *the pot needed a name*, use it. The chickens
in our freezer come directly from the farm of my sister's
college friend. I wonder if they had names, but I'm not that
kind of vegetarian, and my family is not that kind of carnivore. To roast this chicken, put it—fully frozen—into the
slow cooker and set the timer for eight hours. Do this overnight, while you dream, and it's best to do this in the garage so you do not wake to chicken smells in the night. The
timer shuts off the cooking and keeps the chicken warm in
the wee hours, letting it rest and cool, so the juices settle
back into the meat. By the time the morning clears your
mind, the chicken is cool enough to handle, yet still within
safety guidelines for temperature, and the meat slides off
the bones with the barest of pressure from your fingers.
Take your time. Do not forget to find the wishbone to

wash and put on the windowsill to dry, so your small niece and nephew can find it when they visit. Put the meat into one bowl, the bones into the soup pot. The secret to good stock is not to strip the bones too clean—and for all that is chicken and holy, do not rush your stock. Add some carrots, onion, celery. Fill the pot with enough water to cover the bones and turn on the heat, bring it to a boil, then turn it to low. Put the cover on, the satisfying weight of the cast iron, but tilt it just a little. The secret is a bare simmer and time. Ask your resident carnivores to taste your stock, which should darken as the hours move, and ask them to judge it this way: *Would you drink this, on its own, out of a mug you can wrap your hands around, in the chill of a bright winter noon?* Salt will probably be necessary at this point. I do not like to add salt earlier, because the stock concentrates. If you are satisfied with the strength of your stock, strain it and put it back into the pot, or freeze it for later. From here, you can chop and add back your chicken, and if you overcooked the bird as I have done more than once, in the soup it will rehydrate and no one will notice. In the winter, when fresh vegetables are scarce, I rely on a bag of frozen mixed vegetables. Sometimes, I will make dumplings sharp with Parmesan and parsley to cut the mellowness of the soup, a mellowness that comes only from taking your time, the surprise when you lift the heavy lid of the pot and the dumplings have expanded to fill the space. Is this what time tastes like?

When our next-door neighbor brought Jewish penicillin to my mother in the days after her chemo treatments, she told us that this soup in her hands was the product of years of arguing with her husband over whose mother's matzo ball soup is better: *When he makes it,* she says, *he can make it his way.* Science argues that there are indeed measurable health benefits to chicken soup, particularly that which can be traced back to the ground the chicken scratched, a meal full of nutrients a sick body needs, hydration. But science cannot measure the body's need for time, for love, even if it is simply soup for dinner, no illness required, just the act of slowing down long enough to let the soup cool on your spoon.

33

THE BACK OF THE line was a bad place to be on Potluck Sunday at Bethany Lutheran Church in Nevis, because even though my grandmother Phyllis would have made two batches of rice pudding—*risgrynsgröt*—you still might not get any. If you asked, she would share the recipe, but she would tell you, to make it right, *Don't rush it and don't try to substitute ingredients.* If you were lucky enough to get one of her pies at a church bake sale before they sold out, she would tell you that she never made a pie until after she married—and the trick to a flaky crust is cold shortening and cold water. She never used butter or lard in her pies, just shortening, believing in not messing with something that worked. My grandmother's faith was rock solid. She believed in chocolate-chip-cookie care packages and the Minnesota Twins, the Bible and Peterson's *Field Guide to Birds of North America*. Even now, with flurries in the cold Christmas darkness where my grandmother is gone and her only child has been driven into a hospital bed by chemo-therapy, I hear my grandmother's voice whispering James Russell Lowell's "The First Snowfall":

The snow had begun in the gloaming,
And busily all the night
Had been heaping field and highway
With a silence deep and white. . . .

We spend a snowy Christmas Eve in the hospital in a special room for the immunocompromised, and we are all more than a little frightened because my mother has just begun her chemotherapy and cannot manage to stay out of the hospital. I whisper as much of Lowell as I can remember—not usually more than the first two stanzas—and once, when I'd read the entire poem, I stopped with his grief at the end, and vowed just to enjoy the beginning of the poem from now on.

We gather in the waiting room, spreading sparkling juice and store-bought lefse on the table. We wear Santa hats and paste on smiles for my small niece and nephew, my mother wearing a Santa hat to keep her hair from falling out into her eyes, catching on her lips. Her hair is falling out now these short weeks into chemotherapy, layers of filaments on her pillow. But it is not that simple: losing her hair is physically painful, her scalp itself angry and tender against knitted hats. Even this, something that seems passive, hurts more than the soul. Days later, I make rice pudding for our rescheduled Christmas dinner and my mother eats it, the first real food she has eaten in days and I wonder about the miracle of it, that she is eating, that she is eating this particular food. Maybe we shouldn't be surprised.

Just last week, a family friend told a story about her father, who had come to Minnesota from Sweden when he was a small boy. My grandmother found him a kindred spirit. Toward the end of his life, there was a time when he refused to eat and the doctors started talking about a feeding tube to keep him alive. My grandmother, likely unaware that he was dying, brought him a small Tupperware of rice pudding and he ate it. He lived several more years. Another friend said she's made rice pudding for seven friends going through chemotherapy and two pregnant friends and it's the only thing they've been able to eat. My sister was never troubled by morning sickness, which is a miracle in itself, and this pregnancy is no different. She faced mild nausea in each of her first trimesters, but no vomiting, and I am grateful she was spared this complication. There is, however, a photograph of my middle sister and me—I am probably three, my sister eighteen months—crammed into the space between the toilet and the wall, eating crackers with beatific small-child smiles—and what is out of my father's camera range is my mother, hovering over that toilet, pregnant with our youngest sister. We are stealing her crackers. It makes me smile, wondering if my grandmother ever brought my mother rice pudding when she was pregnant.

I like the idea of miracles even as I am skeptical about

the larger concept of who gets the miracles and who does not. But this is a time of year for miracles, for Christmas, the solstice, for belief structures that we create in the dark with the faith that the sun will return. My grandmother believed in many things. Like her, I believe in food for the soul and the miracle of risgrynsgröt.

On my niece's first Christmas, she got her first taste of rice pudding and was not particularly impressed. She was teething, so the large carrot she'd been chewing on was more interesting. My grandmother made the rice pudding that Christmas, making sure that there were enough almonds for each of her now-adult granddaughters to find, so they could make a wish. Originally, the tradition was a dried bean and the one who found it would be the next to be married. These days, because my nephew is allergic to nuts, we have swapped almonds for raisins. This year, I imagine that our risgrynsgröt wishes, the sole miracle we hope for, are all the same.

34

WE ARE "I AM So Glad Each Christmas Eve" people, people of "Stille Nacht" that I remember my grandfather singing in German when I was very young. We are people of darkness and candlelight and anticipation. We are the 1912 country church in Nevis of old wood and old windows on which my pastor father placed votive candles against that encroaching night, the individual candles we held lit for "Silent Night" against my father's standard admonition *not to torch the person in front of you*. The lights in the small sanctuary wink out as the harmony rises.

It was always so warm with body heat and Lutheran harmonies on those Christmas Eve nights, hushed in awe as the last chord echoes up, as the candles are blown out, before the organ blasts the first notes of "Joy to the World" and my mother, sisters, and I belt the alto line at the top of our lungs. Christmas is not a time for silent contemplation. That is the purpose of Advent. I have had enough silence and contemplation in the house in these December days when we have not figured out my mother's nausea medication or her inexplicable fevers or the near-absolute silence of the hospital. As Christmas is now here, I need that boisterous joy, the frenzy of small children, the knowledge of everything how it should be, where it should be, the way I know how to navigate this night where we will leave my mother in the hospital alone. It may be cold here, but we know how to live in this world. Tradition is a solid foundation in an uncertain world where the days shorten and we spend most of our days in darkness, turning on the reindeer and Santa decorations on our lawns, the icicle lights on the eaves, so we know the way home.

35

WE USED TO CALL my grandfather Kermit the Pancake King in the superlative way of children as he stood quietly at the counter on bright summer mornings with his spatula, carefully watching the edges of the batter for the right kind of bubbles, expertly flipping them to golden-brown glory, the same kind of rich light turning the knotty pine of the Cabin's kitchen to maple-syrup gold. It was the kind of morning that makes children think of *Cloudy with a Chance of Meatballs*, the fantasy and magic of sunlight being something we could drizzle over our pancakes.

My grandfather would have pulled a kitchen chair to the counter so that my sisters and I could stand at the right height to watch him, the chair's back forming a cage to keep us from falling. My grandmother would stand near the stove, making frozen summer blueberries into a quick syrup. My grandfather's griddle of choice was electric, as is the griddle we bought for my father as we crowned him the new Pancake King after my grandfather died. Last Christmas, I gave my brother-in-law, M., a cast-iron griddle to keep on their gas cooktop, along with a container of from-scratch pancake mix with an IOU for a refill. "Keep practicing," we'd say with our mouths full, because in our house, Keep Practicing is the best compliment a cook can receive: even if the cake or the pot roast or the tomato soup is the best you've ever eaten, you always tell the cook to Keep Practicing, so they'll keep making it. Keep Practicing, because once perfection is achieved, there is no point in repeating it. We make our own philosophy. Every family does.

In these days of cast iron, where new pieces appear on my thrift store shelves with delightful regularity, I find a dark cast-iron aebleskiver pan, satisfying in its heft, those seven round wells ready for batter to turn into fluffy pancake balls. Aebleskiver are Danish, not Swedish, and not part of our family traditions, but I have been curious about them because our family is so fond of breakfast for dinner. I've rescued two aluminum Nordic Ware aebleskiver pans in the time since, but the cast iron remains my favorite.

On the first attempt at aebleskiver, I deflate most of the stiff egg whites I am directed to fold into the batter. I cannot manage the correct temperature of the pan to cook the batter without burning the outside first, as I look for those tiny bubbles in the batter that my grandfather taught me indicated readiness to flip. My technique of turning the aebleskiver with bamboo skewers will take practice, and I will eventually discover that I like to turn them twice, rather than three times, but there are a few that turn out perfectly golden brown, that kind of buttered crispness holding the entirety together. I figure out how much batter fills the wells and which spoons offer the perfect measurement. Later, when I continue my practice, I find the confidence to fill some with cream cheese. My niece finds herself addicted to lemon curd, and at some point, I should learn to make it because store bought is spendy.

An old friend sends me his family recipe, one that uses one more egg than my previous attempt. Practice makes perfect, but there's also a moment where generational knowledge means something, even if it's not my own generational knowledge. It's one reason I like to rescue old pans—I like the idea that the cook's knowledge is somehow baked or fried or simmered into the pan itself. Days like this, I wish for powers of psychometry. As I practice with this new recipe, I get better at folding in egg whites, as my friend's mother swears by her slotted spoon. This works perfectly when I try. Next time, I add a little cream of tartar to the egg whites to help them retain their air, but the batter still deflates by the time I come to the last ones. This will take more practice. I attempt the nonstick Nordic Ware pan, and while it is easy and the aebleskiver are delicious, they lack the special qualities of the cast-iron pan brushed with melted butter against sticking. My family gently and lovingly informs me that one batch is enough for three people; two batches is barely enough for our family of eight; when, months from now, the four April birthdays—both sisters, my father, and M.—request aebleskiver for their family party, they make sure I know that I will need three batches of batter and I will need all three pans to ensure we can eat in a reasonable time.

Pancakes are magic food to us. I request pancakes for my own birthday each October and we tell my dad to Keep Practicing each time. But this Christmas Eve, my mother is in the hospital for one of her 100.4 fevers and we do not want to leave her there by herself on Christmas, but we have small children who need their beds. My father stays, holding my mother's hand against the impending bone pain of the drugs that will boost her white blood cell count and allow her to go home in a few days. She has had this drug before and the pain of it was excruciating. She knows the pain is coming and she whispers to my father, *I'm afraid*. We do not want to leave her, but we have to. It's Christmas Eve and there is no way to say how awful this is. We stop at Perkins on the way home, my sisters, M., the two kids, and I, and we all order breakfast: pancakes and waffles, the sweet crisp of a fork into the pancakes, syrup deftly divided into waffle wells, the kind of food we need against the exteriors we hardened against the realities of our mother's cancer and Christmas in the hospital, to protect against soft fear and anxiety we carry in our bellies.

36

JANUARY IN MINNESOTA IS color stretched thin, pulled until you can see through it, even the delicate aquamarine too cold to hold clouds. January is the palate cleanser to the density of Midsommar Dag twilight or Fourth of July cobalt. January is the warm side of the color wheel, the male cardinal we call Daddy Red, the stop sign, the orange-yellow of the school bus that would be invisible in summer, blues and greens fading to dark neutrals. There is a clarity in January that summer lacks, this ability to see through color, although because of the phenomenon of Rayleigh scattering, I don't trust the blue in front of me. Even the blue of my mother's eyes is deceiving, as there is no actual blue pigment there. In some senses, blue doesn't exist, the point where green becomes violet on the spectrum indistinguishable in many languages: Where do you find the moment where one thing becomes something else?

The graduated blue of my Cousances Le Creuset Dutch oven is the kind of morning twilight that doesn't quite know day has arrived yet. The deep, saturated color of the pot is similarly graduated, lightest on the bottom, darkest at the top. This is Midsommar Dag blue. This is Yeats's "He Wishes for the Cloths of Heaven" Blue, the "heavens' embroidered cloths, / Enwrought with golden and silver light, / The blue and the dim and the dark cloths / Of night and light and the half-light" kind of blue. The pot's name is Phyllis, after my Swedish grandmother, in the way that I have named all my Le Creuset as they leaped at me from thrift store shelves. I have champagne tastes in cookware and a beer budget, as they say, and the food metaphors are on point today. To recast the insidious mess of cancer in wholesome things, flavors and recipes that bring me good memories, makes me uncomfortable.

This pot is an enameled braiser, a variety of Dutch oven, with little nubs on the inside of the lid so steam can condense and drop back onto whatever is being cooked low and slow. She is a Cousances Le Creuset, Cousances being of the oldest cast iron foundries in France, swallowed up by Le Creuset in 1957. Last night, I made my mother mashed potatoes in that pot as she started to fade from the stress of the past forty-eight hours. This morning, I find the moment—6:46 a.m.—where the night becomes the twilight color of the pot sitting on the stove. There is no line between night and light. Day only becomes in the way that water boils. Yesterday she had her triple cocktail of chemotherapy drugs, then a white blood cell—boosting

drug twenty-four hours later to inspire her stubborn neutrophils, chased with a common over-the-counter allergy
medication to prevent bone pain, and no food sounded
good to her. There is a twilight grace period before she
is unable to get out of bed and we know she needs to eat
something, anything, before that happens, before the
mouth sores, before she has trouble swallowing, before the
dead belly feeling in her midsection, because it will be days
before we can convince her to eat solid food.

We Swedes are, stereotypically, people of bland white
food. My grandmother Phyllis was notorious for thinking
that salt and pepper were pushing it when it came to spices;
she always bought her dill pickles without garlic. We are
people of potatoes, dairy, risgrynsgröt, Christmas cookies
in shades of butter. My grandmother never liked pickled
herring, but her cousins always brought some as a gift for
my German grandfather when they visited. Nobody fought
him for it. In summer, approaching Midsommar Dag, we
dig tender, tiny new potatoes from the garden, boil them
whole, then put them back in the pot with milk and butter,
and serve those red potatoes swimming in rich whiteness
that glimmers with butter fat. *Mjölk och potatis.* In summer,
we feast on color, cucumbers in salt water, corn on the cob,
red potatoes, tomatoes sliced thick. We rarely eat blue, I realize, rarely drink it. Sometimes a Minnesota summer gives
us dark blueberries if we hunt through forests for them,

if we want to rub earth from them instead of buying them encased in plastic. Blue has no scent, in the way that green may smell of mown grass or honeydew. It's documented that blue needs to be taught, that it's the last color to develop in a culture's vocabulary, because we take the sky for granted. I still marvel at the degrees to which blue does not exist, even when we are convinced it does.

37

THE HARALSONS STILL ON the tree in the yard hang
like bells in the strangeness of morning that lightens without source yet still seems like it should ring. It is January, with days longer than December, but somehow seem
shorter and bleaker. The veins and the capillaries of the
apple tree branches are stark against a dreaming-of-pewter
sky, and all I can see is that tree and imagine the port in
my mother's chest fitting into a network just like that one.
This tree is the result of the neighbor's daughter planting
a seed thirty years before from the best Haralson she'd ever
eaten, but she didn't know that if you want a reproduction
of an apple, the tree must be grafted, not planted from
seed. What grew was nearly inedible. My grandmother liked
Haralsons for her apple pies. I think about what the doctors call *seeds* inside my mother's body, the ones that we
can't see, the seeds that are supposed to be that cell, not this
one, what should be grafted to grow and which will grow
rogue and unwelcome. My mother sleeps as morning lightens after yet another late-night ER visit, about the time the
apples on this tree froze and refused to fall, refused to yield

to determined squirrels. It's barely dawn, so I see no color variation between the tree and its apples, which I know are the mottled red-brown of a female cardinal. Come spring, we'll watch the drunk bees stumble in the air.

38

THIS MORNING, MY FATHER complained of a sore throat, which is usually a simple nuisance, one that takes his normal baritone into an absolute bass, but my mother had her Day 1 chemotherapy yesterday, six hours of three caustic poisons. By tomorrow, my mother will lose all ability to fight infection. At noon, my father took to his bed and my nerves tensed until I could hear them in my own ears. My mother has been coughing lately, too, but the CT scan she had two days ago to check the spread of cancer came back with crystal-clear lungs and no cancer. For the first time since my mother's doctor said *cancer*, I am truly afraid, down to my bones, in a way I was not afraid during her surgery, when she started chemotherapy, or when she was unable to get out of bed for days. It is February and the chemotherapy is building in her body and not letting go. It takes longer for her to recover from each infusion, longer for her to make the transition from her bed. What used to be days stretches into weeks. We are only two months into her treatment and the fear that she will not be able to fight off my father's germs chokes me.

Yesterday, my mother's Day 1 infusion happened in the brand-new facility at the University of Minnesota. The staff now walks around with tablets to check in patients; there are no televisions in the individual patient areas. She reports that it feels clinical, rather than comforting and efficient. My mother's body is technically free of cancer cells after her hysterectomy, but we are reminded, many times, that if she does not do chemo, there is a 70 percent chance of recurrence and a 40 percent chance of survival; with chemotherapy, she has a 90 percent chance of survival if it returns. Other friends report they have been given the same statistics, so this is not unique to my mother and her particular cancer. It is in these days that I feel disingenuous when I say my mother has cancer, because even though this treatment is from the deepest depths of Dante's imagination, she will survive. I don't have to worry that I will lose her, barring the unexpected. She doesn't have stage 4 metastatic cancer. We're not worrying about shrinking a tumor or searching for miracles. We have no benchmarks for success and that rubs me raw as I watch her suffer.

I infuse four cups of water, a knob of ginger sliced thin, a quarter cup of honey, and two tablespoons of fresh lemon juice in Penelope Pumpkin. I do not consider closely the chemical properties of the lemon-honey-ginger infusion, beyond *I know this will make him feel better* and *I need to keep him hydrated because he doesn't eat when he's sick.* But honey has been used in medicine for thousands of years; lemons are antibacterial; ginger is anti-inflammatory. There is chemistry here, even if I don't understand it completely.

Chemicals are how we perceive the world, reactions of cells that tell us what we see and what we taste. The incidence of depression in cancer patients—brought on not simply by their diagnosis and prognosis but by the chemical imbalances caused by chemotherapy—seems to make sense. In the days and weeks following her first chemo treatments, my mother underwent a drastic personality shift, snapping orders, making nasty comments, *please* and *thank you* gone from her vocabulary. The change was so worrisome, so much the opposite of who she was, that she specifically asked her palliative doctor about it at their next appointment. He put her on an antidepressant and our mother returned to us.

Day 1 infusion: vincristine, dactinomycin, and Cytoxan. Vincristine will be what causes neuropathy in my mother's hands and feet months from now, so that she cannot walk in her shoes and she hands me the nail clipper because she no longer has the strength in her hands to trim her fingernails. Cytoxan is a mustard gas derivative, and I am thinking of the Second Battle of Ypres in 1915, the first use of mustard gas by the Germans, one hundred thousand left dead, the mustard-ginger-yellow clouds of it destroying the lungs of anyone in its path. Fritz Haber's process that developed the mustard gas is also responsible for ammonia-based fertilizers that turned famine fields into fertile soil, saving millions of lives. In the correct doses, Cytoxan destroys cancer cells, leaving the healthy cells mostly intact. It is a flip of a coin, this moment to harm or heal, to aim the mustard gas at enemy soldiers and not your own and be satisfied with the collateral damage. Can you still win the war—how pervasive the war metaphors of cancer become when the treatment is literally derived from a chemical weapon forbidden by the Geneva Conventions—if you lose all the battles?

I wander the quiet of the house with bleach wipes to clean door handles, the chlorine burning in my nose long after I finish my task. I prepare another batch of the magical ginger tea for my father, the work of my hands the only antidote to the cortisol in my blood. We process fear—the threat of harm—physically, chemically. The amygdala portion of our brain communicates chemically with the parts of our nervous system that produce the fear responses, cortisol and adrenaline. But whether fear is physical or emotional remains a gray area and I must be careful as I peel ginger with hands that shake.

39

THE AIR IS WHITE mint as flakes catch on noses and
eyelashes, a musical expression of that wonderful, magical cellular protein that deserves a more lyrical name than
TRPM8, this blizzard swirling and dipping as if directed by
a conductor's baton. This protein responds only to specific
stimulants, like those found in mint, menthol, and euca-
lyptus, which allows certain ions to change the information the brain receives, the signals it sends to the nervous
system. The effect is that the body is tricked into believing
the mouth is cold. That seems logical enough, even delightful, the wonder of the human body beyond even its
own comprehension. Yet there is a moment in this quiet
whirl of bright snow, as my mother attempts to transfer
from her bed to the couch so I can wash her sheets, because
the chemicals we have pumped into her are leaching out
of her skin, so that we are warned that we should not let
the dog lick to comfort her, and I wonder about chemicals and chemical reactions. I've often wondered why mint
tastes better in the winter, maybe something as simple as an
illusion of heat, that it's cold outside and you're drinking

something warm even as those impish proteins trick the body into feeling a chill. But wintermint rings also of the inability to breathe, of Vicks VapoRub that smells of my grandparents, which my sister now rubs on the bottom of my nephew's feet when he catches a cold. We still cannot figure out much of why the body does what it does, why, even though we can identify the receptors and the proteins and the chemicals that make us feel one way or another, the body can still surprise us.

40

MARCH CAME IN LIKE a lion as leap year offered
an extra day of north wind, my mother's birthday the first
of the month. We are a family of winter-spring birthdays,
starting with my niece and nephew in January-Febru-
ary, my mother in March, and my father, two sisters, and
brother-in-law in April. It is Birthday Season, where we
find color in lurid cake frostings, not the outside world as
we do with the changing leaves for my October birthday.
Two of my favorite Le Creuset pots have been pressed into
service for my mother's birthday dinner: Estelle will make
Julia Child's boeuf bourguignon and Phyllis will make Deb
Perelman's mushroom bourguignon, the comfort food of
thick stew on a cold March evening.

Three days before her birthday, two months after she
requested we shave her head, my mother realized her eyebrows and eyelashes were finally gone. We had been told,
back at the beginning, that chemo attacks fast-growing cells
and that means white blood cells and hair cells, not just
cancer cells. The chemo doesn't know the difference: it
simply destroys the quick. So much of this cancer world

is quick. My mother was scheduled for surgery a week after her diagnosis. Four weeks into her recovery, she met with a sarcoma specialist at the Mayo Clinic, then a sarcoma specialist at the University of Minnesota a few days later. Nobody, including the specialists, wanted to *wait and see*. But we must wait for patterns, for something to repeat so we can understand what it is we are seeing. We watch my mother suffer as the cycles spiral, because we know her doctor cannot discern patterns without time. Her oncologist may know what he is looking for, but we do not, and he does not tell us and we struggle to get the most basic information out of him. I cannot shake the need to reclaim the hours she has lost to treatment. There are days in the kitchen where I want shortcuts, where I want the quick version of bourguignon, but today is not one of those days.

This week, my mother did not receive her Day 8 chemo treatment—*quelle surprise*—because her platelets and potassium were too low. This is not the first—or even the second—time this has happened and nobody has been able to tell me why this is acceptable. On days like this, I need the physicality of cooking: I need the tension of a spatula through a cake batter, I need the action on the surface of a simmer, I need the chop. Days like these, I need to slow down, to take the hours required to make broth and stock, simmering mushrooms, Parmesan rinds, beef bones into something wonderful and useful because one cannot maintain that frustration and anger long term. Sometimes I need to watch the water in the pot reduce, marking time by evaporation. Sometimes I need to be reminded to breathe, to take the long view. So I made the stock for each birthday bourguignon—the beef and the mushroom—from scratch. Something inside me needed to do it. Because it is my mother's birthday and the world is incredibly wrong.

When I went to Hackenmueller's Meats in Robbinsdale, I asked first for stew meat and the young woman behind the counter, energetic in her white apron, asked what I was making and I told her boeuf bourguignon. Julia Child's boeuf bourguignon. I needed six ounces of bacon as well, and she paused, asked again what I was making. *Well, she said, we have bacon, but we also have bacon ends, which might actually be better for what you're doing.* Excellent, I said, grateful in the way that a vegetarian in a butcher shop can be. Next time, as I have consulted several different recipes and techniques, I will simply buy a chuck roast and cut it myself. I won't eat the boeuf bourguignon, but as a cook, I prefer larger chunks of meat in a stew. I deviated from the recipe, because if you watch the boeuf bourguignon episode of *The French Chef* online, the method she follows is not how the recipe is written. (*The French Chef* also does not use onions and carrots, the way the written recipe does.) I'm waiting for the time my mother has lost to reconstitute in this bourguignon, the equivalence of six hours of caustic poisons to be replaced by six hours of food that feeds the rest of who we are, the dark empty spaces inside us, the gathering of family around one table to mark the passage of one year into the next.

41

WE DO NOT THINK in terms of large time anymore, as we have adopted the philosophy of *Just get through today; if that's too much, get through the next hour; if that's too much, the next ten minutes, the next five minutes, the next minute.* Three-week cycles. CT scans every three months. Birthdays, anniversaries, the same menu requested every year, the repetition so comforting simply because it exists. Daylight saving time came this week, but instead of light, it brought rain and a cardinal's cadence from somewhere we couldn't see and I wonder about ancient peoples and how they measured their time, if they thought of time in terms of the full moon's return and the language of light.

The spring equinox next week will bring the snakes back to the staircases of Chichén Itzá in Mexico as my mother returns to Day 1 of her cycle and what else do we have in this season of cancer except to quarter the year, to measure time by light? On the winter solstice two months ago, a day my mother was hospitalized for a fever, the rising sun lit the interior of Newgrange, the five-thousand-year-old passage tomb north of Dublin, a light in the darkest of places on the shortest day of the year. On the spring and fall equinox, light finds its way through the tiny window at San Juan de Ortega in Spain to illuminate the pillar capital carved with the scene of the Annunciation, the angel Gabriel appearing to Mary, and I wonder if he says, *We call them tri-mesters*. On the summer solstice of Midsommar Dag, when my mother's treatment has ended, we will try to convince the children to sleep even though it is bright.

42

IT IS MID-MARCH, TWO weeks after my mother's birthday, which also marks the midpoint of her chemotherapy regimen, and I am instituting the First Annual Holy Week of the Kitchen. This is the place where I fully ignore the ugly food metaphors of cancer and decide that I will create my own damn metaphors. March 14 is π Day—3.14. March 15 is the Ides of March. March 16 is Saint Urho's Day, the feast day of the fictional Finnish saint who drove the grasshoppers from Finland, loudly feted in the small Finn-populated town of Menahga, twenty miles from my hometown. I was well into adulthood before I learned Saint Urho was not real. Holy Week concludes with Saint Patrick's Day, full of vegetarian colcannon, soda bread, Irish cheese and butter, and other Irish delights.

I am making a pot π today. Two pounds of cheap white button mushrooms shred to confetti under the steel blades of my hand chopper. My niece does not like mushrooms, something I often forget, and even though I am not a cook who tries to trick people into eating things, C. told me she doesn't like the way mushrooms feel against her teeth, so I'm experimenting with cutting them so small that it isn't an issue, because it's not the flavor she objects to. On special occasions when I was a kid, my mother would buy frozen potpies to pull out of the freezer when she didn't feel like cooking, so potpies are a treat. My sisters and I always liked the chicken or the turkey; my mother preferred the beef. It might have been the incredible sodium content, because salt is the element that makes food taste more like what it is, but I loved those little potpies, the meat and vegetables, the gravy, the crust. It all worked. There was something truly perfect about them.

I make the filling from mushrooms, sweet potatoes, yams, Yukon Gold potatoes, and carrots, vegetable broth thickened with flour, flavored with garlic and thyme. Pies were originally savory, not sweet, I learn. I put the pot of filling on the back deck to cool while I attempt the pie crust, because it's March in Minnesota and *What do people in warm climates do without this extra space for food*? I have not yet discovered *The Great British Baking Show* and thus I do not know that hot water crust pastry is a thing that exists, though I am starting to understand that the American version of a potpie is much different from the British, one preferring a stew-like consistency to the filling and the other simply laying meat and vegetables inside. I vow that on the next π Day, I will be in possession of the correct tin and a working knowledge of hot water crust pastry. I do not yet know the strength of this kind of pastry, how easy it is to make, how forgiving it is when I don't manage to make it right. I do not yet know that is the kind of pastry I want to build my life with.

I expect epic failure with what I am doing, but I am doing it anyway. About the time the oven reports that it is ready, I line the casserole dish with my grandmother's pie crust, ladling in the now-cool mushroom, vegetable, potato, sweet potato mixture, then top it with the second half of the crust. I pinch it tight at the sides, then poke a pi symbol in the top. There is no way this pie is coming out in one piece, but I have no other options. Into the oven, though I have no idea how long it will take to cook, because I'm operating without a recipe, and it takes about thirty to forty minutes for the crust to achieve that golden-brown glory. At the table, full of laughter, the carnivores don't even notice the lack of meat and my niece doesn't notice the mushrooms. I try not to apologize for what I put in front of them. *No matter what happens in the kitchen, never apologize*, Julia Child says, and today, that's difficult to manage.

There was morning and there was evening and there was pie, the first day. And I looked around the kitchen at what I had created and even though it wasn't perfect, I saw that it was very good.

43

MY BLOND SPRITE OF a niece meets me at her front door: "Kinny, did you bring cookies?" Last week, I'd brought snickerdoodle dough. The time before that, it was chocolate chip cookie dough. The family has a history of cookies and children: my grandmother Phyllis sent us chocolate chip cookies in our college care packages, and before that, for the first Christmas after they were married, my father gave my mother a Cookie Monster cookie jar. My mother was not exactly thrilled. But then she opened her present from her mother-in-law, my grandmother Marion, who had given her lingerie. She wanted grandchildren.

"Even better," I tell C. "I brought Agnes." H. simply bounces next to her, beside himself with excitement. If hope is a thing with feathers, then delight stands in the sunshine blowing bubbles. Delight is visceral, the energy of love. It's nerves in the stomach; it's pride expanding the rib cage. This is where laughter comes from. Is it any wonder, then, that the joy of baking feeds us in this way?

We will use Agnes to make an apple galette to celebrate Pi Day. C. and H. pull their chairs to the counter, already in their bright aprons made by my mother when C. was two, the backs of the chairs a cage to prevent them falling backward. I ask C. if she remembers how to measure flour and there's pride in my belly when she says yes, remembers to tap the flour on the top of the cup with the back of the knife to settle it, then level it off. My grandmother was not a baker who weighed her ingredients. She would have considered it fussy, so even though I know the good reasons to weigh flour, I still teach C. the method my grandmother taught me. *Okay,* I say, *I need two cups of flour,* and I leave her to it. C. is tall for her age, slender, and sarcastic. When we were teaching her to say *please* around the age of two, she created her own neologism of "May you please . . ." as in "May you please bake cookies with me?" There are days when I ache a little at the loss of language these children have created, the days when my nephew will say *I love you* instead of *I yuv you,* when the dog's name is *Lucy,* not *Yucy,* when C.'s diction is perfect. We create our world through our mouths, first through food. It is our entry into a world outside ourselves. Later, we create our world through the language of our mouths, our hands.

I ask C., *What happens when you mix oil and water?* For her last birthday, she got a science kit full of experiments, most of which involved vegetable oil, so she knows that oil and water won't mix. When I tell her butter is fat and it won't mix with the water we'll add later, this is a moment of food science that she understands, that little brow-furrowed thinking expression on her face as she digests the information, makes the connection, and files it away in that remarkable brain of hers to be resurrected at odd moments.

I teach the niblings, not just because it's fun, but because I want them to grow up with these memories—cooking with Aunt Kinny is *something we do*. We are not a *Children should be seen and not heard* family. More often than not, when I babysit or when I pick her up from the bus, C.'s first question is *Can we bake something?* I teach her that we cook to Aretha Franklin, nobody else, a signal to others as they walk in the door that if we're belting out "Baby I Love You" or "I Knew You Were Waiting" that something awesome is in the oven—and when H. is old enough, we'll give him a spatula for a microphone and his own verses to sing. We, simply, find these particular children to be delightful, clever creatures that we genuinely like to be around. They are smart, they are empathetic, they are funny.

For my great-grandmother Florence, pie baking was a chore; she baked five or six pies every day to feed the threshers during harvest during the Depression and I do not imagine she enjoyed it. My grandmother would remind us that she never made a pie until she married, partly because of the family dynamics of an alpha mother and older sister and partly because of her new life as a housewife, having lost her teaching job when she married in 1948. For my grandmother, making pie became an act of love, something she did by heart, to know that thing well enough that it became part of our emotional systems, not simply the practical. Our Thanksgivings were capped by apple pie, sometimes blueberry, but never pumpkin. This idea of Pi Day, this is something my grandmother would have known by heart and by hand, the knowledge there in her body, the repetition of rolling pins so automatic that she would know everything she needed to know about that crust simply by the press of her finger in the way that I can touch the surface of a cake and know if it is done. The historical knowledge of the body is something we often take for granted, the knowing in our bones, our skin. And so I am working to create new historical memories with my niece and nephew, writing the new food history of our family.

44

CANCER DIVIDES—AS ITS VERY premise, its cells divide, maniacally, so that one rogue cell becomes two becomes a three-pound cabbage-sized tumor. Yet the same is happening inside my sister in a different way, as her child who was once one cell became two cells is becoming a brand-new human being we cannot wait to meet. Cancer divides us into those who know what cancer means and those who must use our very best imaginations to put ourselves inside the figure of our mother unable to move from that couch, midsections deadened by chemotherapy, scalps bare to the world. The divisions are everywhere, to the point where I can watch continents drift if I stand in one place long enough, and I want to hold hard against things that should not be. Her oncologist talks about "localized recurrence" *if* it comes back—because they still call her "cancer free"— and I go back to what they told us about chemotherapy at the beginning, that "cancerous tumors are characterized by cell division, which is no longer controlled as it is in normal tissue. 'Normal' cells stop dividing when they come into contact with like cells, a mechanism known as contact inhibition. Cancerous cells lose this ability. Cancer cells no longer have the normal checks and balances in place that control and limit cell division." I fear that distance, that division. I feel that tension in my core muscles, tightened, my hands closing to fists against the fear that I'll let go—*Beware the Ides of March!* So I go back to the stove on this March 15, to watch pecorino Romano cheese emulsify with pasta water and pepper into *cacio e pepe* in my shallow red Le Creuset pot named Poppy, hoping that it will come together, that it will not separate itself back into its component parts as long as I whisk hard enough, waiting for the family to arrive for dinner and laugh at my table set without knives in honor of Caesar and Brutus, to surround this round oak table in my mother's dining room, a table where her father did his homework in the light of an oil lamp and the warmth of his own mother's kitchen.

45

TURN THE OVEN TO 375 and put Agnes in to preheat. If you are making more than one batch of pannekoeken, put the other cast-iron skillets in to preheat as
well: the eight-inch skillets, like Agnes, feed two people;
the six-inch skillets feed one person. The trick to making
a Finnish pancake, or a Dutch baby, or a pannekoeken, is
in having the pan screaming hot. If it is not hot enough,
it will not create steam in the batter fast enough and your
Finnish pancake will not rise. It is March 16, and the Finns
are celebrating Saint Urho's Day as I celebrate the third day
of Holy Week of the Kitchen. Beat together the flour, milk,
eggs, and salt. I have learned that air in the batter is not
essential to the rise of the pancake: this is not aebleskiver.
You can double or triple the recipe with no effect on the
finished product. When the oven and pans are hot enough,
add your butter to the pans and let it melt. Pour the batter in slowly, so it does not touch the sides of the pan. If
you leave the pans on the oven rack to do this, you will not
have to manage hot skillets of thin, pale batter back into the
oven. Close the oven door and bake for twelve to fifteen

minutes. Do not open the oven door to check its progress. Use the oven light, so you do not let out the heat. The concept of this kind of pancake is the same as a popover: a mix of egg, flour, and milk applied to an incredibly hot pan. Once you master one recipe, you'll have already mastered the other without trying.

Maybe I should have known there was something strange about Saint Urho when nobody outside northern Minnesota knew what I was talking about on March 16. Maybe I should be more embarrassed than I am about being so sucked into this story that I believed it was true. After all, there's a statue of Saint Urho in Menahga, and they crown a king and queen every Saint Urho's Day. Saint Patrick, who is celebrated one day later, drove all the snakes from Ireland—so why was it so hard to believe that another saint had done the same with grasshoppers? One was as unlikely as the other, but most of the saints' stories are fairly unrealistic. All cultures have hero myths, ordinary people who did extraordinary things. Sometimes we just need a hero to help us understand why things are the way they are, beyond our logic and understanding, a moment where we can believe in the impossible.

46

WHEN YOU SPEND ENOUGH time with a potato, you learn the differences between waxy and starchy by feel and instinct, not trivia. Sometimes the only way to know something is by doing, by experiencing the success and failure of the thing yourself. You learn that it's perfectly logical to have both in the darkness of your pantry-closet in containers labeled *boil 'em, mash 'em, stick 'em in a stew* in bold black letters, so that you grab the Yukons for the potato corn chowder you're making with today's Parmesan broth, because you like the way your niece's face lights up when you tell her you're making her favorite soup. You want them to hold, firm. You're not sure where this deep love of potatoes came from, the Hasselbacks, the gnocchi, the potatoes gleaned from the farms around your hometown in the fall to be made into lefse for the holidays.

Russets, baked in the microwave, make an excellent meal when you just can't manage anything more. Multi-colored fingerlings are fun, roasted with sweet Walla Walla onions. You've spent enough time in Ireland—and in Irish literature—to know the history and the delicacy of this

Peruvian export, how this efficient plant came to feed millions, only to be felled by a fungus exacerbated by Ireland's monoculture and climate shifts caused by the Little Ice Age. You've read Michael Pollan and others; you know that the potato monoculture in this country runs the same risk, even as you know that your hometown soil is perfect for potatoes, the potato plant in Park Rapids smelling of french fries destined for McDonald's, the food of our home also intended for someone else. Far from being boring, this simple food taken for granted in its simplicity holds endless complication.

You peel six medium russets on this Saint Patrick's Day, the final day of Holy Week of the Kitchen, two for each of you, and set them to parboil for five minutes, then set them to cool for five minutes on the counter, the steam turning the air opaque as the outer layer of the potato dries out, just a bit. You want the starchy potatoes, not the waxy. Meanwhile, your mustard-colored enameled Descoware casserole named Padraig heats with the 375-degree oven. Mix the potatoes with olive oil, salt, and pepper to coat, then add to the hot cast iron. It sizzles in a way that is deeply satisfying and you shake the pan to distribute evenly. Smoked garlic powder is magical here, but you've learned that it burns, so you'll sprinkle it on at the end. You set the timer for twenty minutes, then come back to turn the potatoes, to shake the pan to cover them in oil so they brown nicely, and back in for three more cycles of twenty minutes. The result is perfect roasties that are golden crispy on the outside, fluffy and perfect on the inside. You could make a meal out of this, you think as you tuck in, thinking also about the rare strength your mother has to sit at the table tonight. She has not been to the table in days.

But this potato has a dark, deadly history, a Peruvian uprooting, deaths of millions of people in a kind of culinary genocide as a million Irish starved and another million emigrated. Even though there was still enough food in Ireland to feed the population, the British hoped that An Gorta Mór would finally finish off the pesky Irish they'd been trying to get rid of for hundreds of years. There's the dark greed of American agribusiness, the moment when agri-culture became agri-business, as Paul Gruchow once wrote. There is darkness here, even as we approach the equinox and the return of the light: in a few months, when your mother's chemotherapy is ended, you'll quarter red new potatoes, boil them, toss with crispy-steamed green beans, and mix with a balsamic-Dijon-lemon concoction so good that you and your sisters will stand in the kitchen eating out of the bowl with your fingers.

47

MAYBE A RAINY SPRING morning happens this way, thunder that cracks like eggs, rain that pounds at a frequency my brain reads as *Go back to sleep*. My mother, in bed for the fourth day after her last chemotherapy treatment, listens to a Louis L'Amour audiobook on her phone as she dozes. There have been many good days in the last four months, but this is not one of the good days. Each treatment continues to hit my mother harder and she takes longer to get out of bed, she takes longer to recover from the *dead belly*. April was the hardest lesson for my mother, that moment where she realized that mind over matter was a terrible lie. It didn't matter how much she tried; she couldn't get up. She couldn't force herself to eat. She certainly could not force herself out of the house to do normal things, to babysit her grandchildren, to sing in the church choir as she always had. Other people could live an approximation of their lives before cancer, but she couldn't. Since she had been "cancer free" since her surgery and this chemotherapy was preventative, the fact of her suffering seemed even crueler. But this is the way we think about illness, about suffering, about crucibles, the goal of which is to come out on the other side with some sort of transcendent knowledge, a revelation, an epiphany, an arc toward recognizing how different we are now from who we were before cancer. But that's ridiculous. We want that bright shining epiphany, but we don't get it. I don't know why we expect it, but we do. Anything that hurts this much, we think, should come with some sort of insight as a reward from the universe. So we keep waiting.

48

THEN CAME THE DAY when I learned that cast iron is not indestructible, the day I turned the heat too high, too fast, under my very old Alfred Andresen *plättpanna* pancake pan. This was not the epiphany I had hoped for. The crack sounded like an explosion in the kitchen, loud, sharp, shards of sound making dents in the walls. Everything froze as we assessed that nothing had actually detonated, there was no damage to anything in the kitchen, and we tried to figure out what had made the noise. Finally, we narrowed it to the pan on the heat, recently washed and heating to remove the last of the water before I swiped it with oil. I could see the crack, down the center of the pan that had survived more than a hundred years of little Swedish pancakes. I hadn't had the pan long, just long enough to research the company, a Minneapolis foundry catering to Scandinavian immigrants, which folded in 1913. I had just figured out the best temperature to make pancakes without burning them and it was not too much to say that I was in love with this pan. It brought me indescribable joy. I wanted to make nothing but pancakes for two solid weeks, wishing for my grandfather to stand over my shoulder and give me his quiet advice. I experimented, basking in the absolute delight of them, how easy it was to buzz up the batter with my immersion blender and pour it from the measuring cup. How it became just as easy to make pancakes on a weekday morning as it was to pour cold cereal. How I discovered the brilliance of my favorite red silicone spatula for the task of flipping the silver dollar–sized beauties back into their wells, how I needed to do it slowly, so as not to make a mess when I flipped them. I learned how much batter to put in each well for them to cook properly. How I should melt butter and use my silicone brush, not just to grease the pan, but also to swipe on the pancakes as they finished cooking, because a knife full of butter would tear the delicate pancakes. I had just started to understand this pan. And then it was gone.

49

MY MOTHER ESCAPED NEUROPATHY until April. Her oncologist asked her to walk on her heels and she could not raise the balls of her feet to do so, so he removed the vincristine from her chemotherapy recipe and told her that the neuropathy should reduce on its own. Probably. From the laurelwood rocking chair in the living room, my father tells my mother that his neuropathy feels like burning, like nerves firing and misfiring and friendly firing in his feet. In his hands and arms, half will go numb at a time. My mother, reclining on the couch under her electric throw, nods. My father's late mother had neuropathy; his aunt K., at age ninety-three, will say, with a twinkle, "When I feel like I'm going to fall, I aim for something soft, push my Life Alert, and four strong, handsome men come to pick me up." My mother's friend F. calls with news that she's missed several of her cancer treatments because of the neuropathy. At the Mayo Clinic, where we have gone for a second opinion on my father's neuropathy, the doctor snaps a tuning fork against his hand, tells my father to close his eyes, and then touches the tuning fork to my father's foot, his ankle, his shin. "Feel the buzz?" he asks. Sometimes my father says yes, sometimes he says no. We are a family of musicians, my mother a pianist so talented that these months of her silent piano seem incredibly wrong. A440—the pitch standard to which instruments are tuned—means something to us.

A lack of B_{12} can damage the nervous system as well as affect the brain functions, with a higher incidence of depression, memory issues, and general fatigue. Perhaps this is the root of how nerves came to be both physical and mental, the physical location in the body of some emotional or personality excess—or lack of fortitude. With amusement, I hear Mrs. Bennet's lament to her husband: "You have no compassion on my poor nerves!" and Mr. Bennet's quipped reply: "You mistake me, my dear. I have a high respect for your nerves. They are my old friends. I have heard you mention them with consideration these twenty years at least." Even Jane Austen knew how emotional nerves are gendered, how my mother's nerves are considered emotional in ways that don't apply to my father's nerves. The doctor is convinced that my father's neuropathy is genetic—and it will continue to progress—so there's very little he can do to prevent more damage. The doctor is surprised that my father has never smoked, and since alcohol can affect nerves, he tells my father that he is allowed only one drink a week. When we get home, I take a bottle of Shiner Bock out of the fridge and use it to make bread in my cast-iron skillet.

We arrive home and I put my pot named Phyllis on the front burner to simmer soup for dinner, that gorgeous cheerful shade of cobalt blue—Co—and I think about how cobalt is part of B_{12}. I wonder if I could form an entire alphabet of neuropathy if I tried, if this is a new language I can create and put on the table. Sometimes I think that the Miracle of Modern Medicine should shield us from this kind of inherited pain, the long-term kind, the kind that prevents us from going about our days doing the things we love to do. But that is not the way of the world, and that is not the way of chronic diseases, because we do not talk about neuropathy or ALS or MS or any other debilitating disease in the same way we do cancer. We don't say my father should fight harder against his neuropathy. Perhaps we need to build our vocabulary from scratch, to shift our metaphors, to build sound from silence in the way the planet spins itself into mornings that turn the snow from blue to white, muffling the outside so my mother can sleep off her chemotherapy in peace, the way my mother's piano remains silent, absent her fingers, mine.

50

AT SOME POINT, ALL nerves get old. The body cannot regenerate in its accustomed ways. They talk about the cumulative effect of cancer treatment, how it takes longer to recover as the chemotherapy builds in the tiniest places in the body, in the nerves, in the white blood cells; what took three days for my mother to recover some sense of normalcy now takes ten days. We think of this, now, as normal, because my mother is sixty-six years old, not as young as she once was, and this is cancer, this is chemotherapy. This is what we should expect. But even young nerves can be abused, never to recover, the perfection of a child's bones and nerves and skin damaged permanently. My father stepped on glass when he was a child and the nerve damage on the bottom of his foot meant we could not tickle him there, no matter how often he danced his fingers over the soles of our feet. As the result of a Buck knife and an onion while camping, I've lost feeling on the inside of my left thumb, unless I hit it directly, and then the pain is excruciating. But we have been raised in *mind over matter*, the battle metaphors of cancer, the fighting, that if you believe hard enough, deep enough, right enough, if your faith is strong enough, you can make your body do what you want. And I wonder about emotional nerves, battered and scarred to a point beyond recovery. Certainly the force of will can be incredible, like the teenage sister of my high school best friend diagnosed with stage 4 bone cancer determined to walk down the aisle at her wedding. She did. Fifteen years later, my friend named her daughters in her sister's memory.

51

I WANT TO BELIEVE that the secret to wild rice is in knowing the lake it came from in northern Minnesota and the name of the man or woman who harvested it, by hand, in the traditional way of the Ojibwe, out in a canoe, bending the stalks over the gunwales and whacking them with sticks called knockers. Wild rice is sacred to the Ojibwe in ways that I, as a white person, can never truly understand and should not be able to understand. Though we are Swedish-German, it's sacred in a different way to us as Minnesotans who grew up here. For my birthday, I always request the Mahnomin Porridge recipe from Hell's Kitchen in Minneapolis, the wild rice, cream, maple syrup, hazelnuts, and cranberries, mixed in Estelle by one of my sisters, while my father flips lemon ricotta pancakes. Last year, we added dried blueberries to the porridge and agreed they were to be part of the new permanent recipe. My father, who once went with friends to learn how to harvest wild rice in the traditional way, requests wild rice for his birthday dinner.

This particular rice came from Lake Garfield in

Hubbard County, and I think of the miracle and science of those canoes on the water. Wild rice has become a part of our family history, that moment between the sacred and the quotidian, this food that is an indicator plant of the health of the watershed. If a lake or river is polluted, the wild rice will not grow. My mother is also an ecosystem under threat, but tonight we pile her wide, shallow bowl high with wild rice, lay pats of butter to melt, and sprinkle lightly with salt, an offering to the forces inside her body to be merciful.

52

TODAY IS MOTHER'S DAY. An incredibly robust robin sits on the railing of the deck, balancing a distended belly of red, and I wonder if this robin will lay her blue eggs in the nest they've been building in the gutter. This national holiday of Woodrow Wilson's, made cliché by Hallmark, makes me more uncomfortable than usual, simply because I have been thinking about mothers and children, about womanhood and femininity, gender and sexuality, nearly every day for the last six months, and I am more skeptical than usual about a day set aside to celebrate fertility, a day to perform the correct kind of motherhood. When I was young, one of the women in our church brought small containers of purple Johnny-jump-ups for the Sunday school kids to give to their mothers, and there's a bit of childhood glee to remembering how excited we were to have a day to love our mothers just a little bit more. B. and her husband never had children and I think about that.

We still remain a society that places a woman's value on her offspring, even beyond arguments about contraception and abortion, to the point where many doctors will not tie a woman's tubes when she asks for it while performing vasectomies without issue, a fact that is complicated by the historical memory of forced sterilizations of women in the early twentieth century. We remain a society that feels the need to have opinions on whether a woman is too old for children, too young for children, or too poor for children. All those years ago, we gave Nadya Suleman the nasty nickname of *Octomom*, feeling it our collective societal right to have an opinion. We judge women on the size of their baby bumps, considering their bodies a canvas for public commentary. We feel entitled to touch their bellies. We comment on how fast a woman returns to her pre-baby body. Just today, though, I read an article about women using climate change as a reason for choosing not to have children, as if we need more justification than *no, thank you* to the question. Today, I struggle against Mother's Day even as I am more grateful than I can say that my mother is here, she is alive, and she is wonderful, and my sister is here with her children, and that is wonderful.

53

ON THE STOVE, PENELOPE Pumpkin waits to simmer a pile of rich red rhubarb into sauce. It's the season for rhubarb, this early May, days when we would pull strawberry-colored stalks from our garden when I was growing up. You pull the rhubarb; you do not cut it from the ground with a knife. Both sides of my family have rhubarb in their repertoires, though an enduring argument of my parents' forty-year marriage is whether one uses cornstarch or tapioca to thicken the sauce. My mother's childhood—and most of mine—was marked by simple Sunday toast-and-sauce suppers, as Sunday's main meal was at noon, and my sisters and I had the choice of the jars in the pantry that we had canned the summer before, the pale applesauce, the peaches, the dark cherries.

We will freeze much of our spring rhubarb for seasons of scarcity, for seasons of great celebration. Christmas mornings and birthday brunches ring in shades of my mother's classic rhubarb-studded Bundt cake, a recipe that lives in the *breakfast* section of my recipe box, not *dessert*. The rhubarb would have been frozen at the peak of its early-summer color and there's a note on my recipe card to drain the rhubarb—otherwise we get mush. My mother's Nordic Ware Bundt pan is liberally greased. My mother's original pan is in the classic shape, perfect for rivers of powdered sugar frosting, but we bought her the Bavaria pan several years ago, which might be even better. I do not even consider choosing a different pan from my now-ludicrous collection of cake pans, which I have acquired in my thrift store hunting. When I see familiar shapes on *The Great British Baking Show* or in the giant bakery case at the Minnesota State Fair, I get a little thrill knowing the actual names of the pans they're using, even as I am mildly embarrassed to possess such knowledge.

Celebrating my mother on this day seems both absolutely necessary and not nearly enough, because we have been acutely conscious of losing her, even thinking back to September and my California grandmother's unexpected death after a fall, our travel to the funeral, and when this season of love and loss started. We think of the heart as the center of love in our bodies, the physical engine that powers our lives, the internal part that represents both the physical and emotional—and we like to believe that we do have inside us the representation of both.

When my niece draws hearts on pink construction paper and colors them red, we know the hearts inside our bodies are not that shape or that rhubarb-red color, but we praise her art with enthusiasm. The heart has no nerves to feel, and yet we speak in metaphors about broken hearts and broken-heart syndrome, like we need to be able to point to a particular place that hurts, that feels filled with love to bursting. It's the language of the figurative that helps us with the physical, because despite our multimillion-year history as humans, we still cannot figure out how to articulate the ways our bodies navigate the world. Heart disease is the number one killer of women, but even now almost all of the research and treatment has been on men, which means that women don't recognize their symptoms as a heart attack. We gather around this rhubarb Bundt cake, my mother at the table, the fuzz of her hair beginning to grow back after she decided it was time to stop shaving it, my father, my sisters and M. and me, my niece and nephew, my sister's hand on her belly as her child kicks and squirms and lodges his or her elbow or knee under her rib cage and pushes as if to remind us *We are here and that is enough for today.*

54

TODAY, *JULIA AND JACQUES COOKING AT HOME* by Julia Child and Jacques Pépin fell off the top of the refrigerator and onto my head. There was no lasting damage to cranium or cookbook, only a flash that this is, perhaps, a terrible place to store cookbooks. Setting it back on its bookshelf between *Thug Kitchen* and the fifth edition of *Cook Boldly* from Holden Village, I realize the brilliance in the world's great cooks and cookbooks is in their ability to explain to me why I should do what they are asking me to do. When competition shows became more popular, I stopped watching the Food Network and started collecting cookbooks and my favorites on this precarious high shelf are the product of deliberate attention, souvenirs from travel, like the *Best Recipes from the Maritime Provinces*, bought at the maritime museum in Halifax, Nova Scotia; or hometown hero Amy Thielen's *The New Midwestern Table*, which contains my favorite sour cream raisin pie from Third Street Market in Park Rapids; or others rescued from thrift stores among the *Cook Yourself Thin* and *The Fat-Burning Bible* that prey on our dissatisfaction with who we're told to be, books that reinforce the morality we've assigned to food and our time in the kitchen.

I keep coming back to Susan Sontag, who writes,

> Disease occurs in the *Iliad* and the *Odyssey* as supernatural punishment, as demonic possession, and as the result of natural causes. For the Greeks, disease could be gratuitous or it could be deserved (for a personal fault, a collective transgression, or a crime of one's ancestors). With the advent of Christianity, which imposed more moralized notions of disease, as of everything else, a closer fit between disease and "victim" gradually evolved. The idea of disease as punishment yielded the idea that a disease could be particularly appropriate and just punishment.

I wonder what she would say about these cookbooks and that the morality and metaphor of cancer and disease has not changed much since she wrote *Illness as Metaphor* in 1978. I look at my bookshelf, where *Fika*, full of Swedish cakes and sweets, offers a promise that if you cook with this book, you will learn to slow down. *Bundt Cake Bliss* promises happiness. These cookbooks promise miracles, not understanding. If I cook with this book, I will be skinny and happy. If I follow these recipes in *The Cancer Survival Cookbook*, my mother will survive her cancer.

Here's why this matters: my friend's wife died. Suddenly, unexpectedly, devastatingly, and everything stopped under the force of a grief that was not mine. This was not supposed to happen. Her ovarian cancer had come back after twenty years in remission about the same time as my mother was diagnosed, and her surgery, two months before, had left her with complications, but she had been strong enough for her first chemotherapy three days ago. She collapsed in her bedroom and was gone before help arrived. I have faith, but I haven't been to church in years. It's not that I don't believe in miracles, or that I'm not comforted by Saint Augustine's famous *If you understand it, it's not God*. I need to believe in patterns beyond my human understanding. But I don't believe in *God's got a plan* or *Everything happens for a reason* or *God doesn't give you more than you can handle* or *Let go and let God*, because the God I believe in is not that cruel. With cancer, faith often becomes a platitude, brightly colored meme-prayers on social media I find viscerally distasteful. We don't give those memes to other chronic diseases. I don't believe in the Miracle of Modern Medicine either, because there's blind faith in medicine, too, and that seems just as cruel and capricious as other belief systems. So I put my trust in Rose Levy Berenbaum's *The Cake Bible* instead.

55

THE PORK ROAST RESTS on paper towels on the counter while Minnie, my three-quart flame-colored Descoware, heats on the stove. Julia Child taught me that if meat is not dry, it will not properly brown. Alton Brown taught me to oil the meat, not the pan. I believe in this braised pork shoulder recipe of Jamie Oliver's, which has never failed me. *Faith without works is dead*, I think as I slice onions with the careful precision of one who has terrible knife skills and the scars to prove it. C. S. Lewis tried to answer *Why do bad things happen to good people?* in *A Grief Observed* after his wife died of cancer. When he writes, "Talk to me about the truth of religion and I'll listen gladly. Talk to me about the duty of religion and I'll listen submissively. But don't come talking to me about the consolations of religion or I shall suspect that you don't understand," that is also where I am today as I return from my friend's wife's funeral. The only thing I know right now is that I know nothing except that the beauty of braising pork like this is in knowing why this cut of meat is the best choice for low and slow, how the connective tissue needs to be broken down so that it can dissolve into the meat and make it soft enough not to aggravate my mother's mouth sores. I do not know any more about this cookbook of cancer than when we started, the *recipe* for the three-drug *cocktail* my mother's doctor prescribed, the food metaphors of cancer coming up hard against how I have been taught to understand the way the world works, and so, instead of C. S. Lewis's *The Problem of Pain* or *A Grief Observed*, I pull James Beard's *Theory and Practice of Good Cooking* from the shelf, curl my knees up to my chest as I settle on the love seat in the sun, and read about the theory and practice of braising.

56

IT SEEMS OBVIOUS THAT fruits and vegetables are
more effective than processed food in giving a body the
tools it needs to fight, that I should feed my mother *food*,
rather than *supplements*, to make sure her body has all the
vitamins and nutrients it needs, even as this is another moment where Susan Sontag's war metaphors of cancer come
up against the food metaphors I have been cooking against.
But my mother has not been fighting any harder than my
friend J.'s wife, and I stare at *The Cancer Survival Cookbook*,
bought mostly as a joke, and I stand there on the day I return from her funeral, frozen in the wash of irrational anger. Cancer. Survival. Cooking.

The idea of A Good Death persists. We still believe
we deserve to die in our sleep, surrounded by loved ones,
with something wise as our last words. We somehow believe
that pain-free old age is a right—but for whom is it an actual reality? Maybe this idea comes from *The Cancer Survival
Cookbook*s of the world, antiaging creams, dye to cover gray
hair, even as these products convince us that age is something that we can avoid, if we're clever. And then we start

thinking about a good life as something we deserve, because we are good people, and we subscribe to the prosperity gospel—or we look at suffering as something God does to make us stronger, to test us, but there is little in the world of illness and cancer philosophy that makes me angrier than that line of thinking. Years ago, I had a student with glioblastoma who dropped out halfway through the semester on his doctor's advice to avoid stress and he told me he was going to spend what little time he had left giving back, volunteering. He still died. He was twenty-two. There's nothing good about that.

How have we assigned a morality to cancer that we have not given to other diseases? How is it that we've come to see cancer as a fundamentally unacceptable way to die, with this morality that we've assigned to it, so if you smoke and you end up with lung cancer, you get what you deserve, but if your spouse who's never smoked a day in her life ends up with lung cancer, that's just *wrong*? Or that discrepancies in health care have come to decide who lives and who dies? The injustice of it is all consuming. The Miracle of Modern Medicine is as arbitrary as miracles offered by the divine: some people are saved and some people aren't. The only thing I believe in right now is in the sweetness of the pork and apple and fennel taking over the house, filling the darkest corners of grief for my friend in his loss, the fists I clench against the injustice of everything, today a world of

unknowing that is capricious and sinister. I place my faith
in old church cookbook recipes titled "Never Fail," today
of all days, when we hold tight to the vehemence of *I love you*
and that *what remains are these: faith, hope, and love, and the greatest
of these is love.*

57

YEARS AGO, IN THE wild of Oakland Cemetery in
Atlanta, the woman in the visitors office hands me a pam-
phlet of information and asks if I'd like to take the Yankees home with me. I do not believe she is joking. This is a
graveyard of historical significance, of Civil War battles, of
segregated burial plots for Christians and Jews, whites and
African Americans, Yankees and Confederates. I wander
this cemetery, thinking of Diane Ackerman, who writes of
that moment in human evolution when the brain "began
storing information outside itself, on stone, papyrus, paper, computer chips, and film" and I rub my fingers over
lichen-crusted stones, trying to clear the dates and names.
My friend J., with whom I share an affection for cemeter-
ies, believes that in the matter of storytelling, silence is not
always a failure: we must respect the choice to stay silent
where such exists in a story. Right now, as he grieves his
wife, the distance between sound and silence is important.
Poet Mark Doty posits that if there are gaps in certainty,
in memory, let that be a part of the telling. These graves,
here, however, grow wild with rosemary, the pine-sweet of

it warm in the air. Rosemary is for remembrance, Ophelia said, and I crush a leaf between my fingers, rub the oils to warm them, and I wonder about the kitchen garden I grow on the deck at home, the pots of basil and cilantro and lavender and rosemary, the rosemary that is my favorite flavor of all, and I wonder about cooking memories into food, about that moment when if I feed my mother bone broth to fix her bones, can I achieve the same as a vegetarian if we consume the rosemary of remembrance? What do we hope to remember and what do I hope will disappear into unfathomable memory because much of these last months I do not want to remember?

58

ON THE OUTSIDE OF the kitchen window, the perfect imprint of a bird in flight, stretched full, larger than my hand. Each feather is perfect, delineated from the next, two wings, a tail, the head, the beak. The bird print is in profile, its head pointing west, wings pointing to soil and sky. The image has the quality of a ghost in a photographic negative: if you change your angle even the smallest degree, the bird disappears, the clarity of its face, the sharpness of beak, the precision of feather, as though you'd imagined it. I have hope that the bird who left this print on my mornings flew away. For this we believe in things we cannot see, for our eyes are on the sparrows at the feeders along the fence as they scatter at the wing of Cooper's hawks who live nearby. My mother sleeps down the hall, her body stunned by chemotherapy. It does not matter that there are no cancer cells to attack. The bird does not know that the window is there. But the glass remembers.

59

Yesterday, my mother talked with her friend
F., who is going through chemo and radiation for breast
cancer.

> *I don't know if I'm going to color my hair when this is all over,* F. said.
>
> *Me, either,* my mother said. *I earned this hair.*

My mother has always had the most incredibly thick
curly blond hair, the kind that led to ironing it straight
in college with actual clothing irons. She didn't have the
tight ringlets she passed on to my middle sister, or the
looser curls of my youngest sister, but thick, wavy curls.
My hair has always resisted any shape but straight. Back
in November, I bought her a fancy coffee at Caribou
Coffee and we went to Great Clips for a free Kindness
cut, so when her hair started to fall out, it wouldn't be
so traumatic for her. Or at least that was the idea. I wondered what it meant when pictures of my mother with
hair looked odd. Her new driver's license has her without
hair. I could see her face so clearly like this, her bright
blue eyes magnetic. My father offered to shave his head in
solidarity, but she told him no. Society is much crueler to

women with thinning hair than we are to men, though we are not kind to them either.

We stopped shaving her in April and she had grown a passable pixie style by the middle of May, her hair growing just as fast as it had before vincristine caused it to fall out. I thought she looked magnificent with such short hair. In its briefness, her hair hasn't started to curl yet, but it's growing in shades of ash blond, brown, silver, and the color changes in different angles of light. It is a magical color, whatever color it is. I tell her that people pay a lot of money for that kind of hair color and she isn't entirely convinced. But I watch her hair grow, watching the visibility of her cancer disappearing with her scalp, with that birthmark, and I watch my mother coming back to herself, out of the shades of a cancer winter of white and gray and sleep and curtains pulled tight.

60

TURN THE OVEN TO 500 degrees and assemble the ingredients: this will go very quickly. On the counter, the last of our winter's store of beef, though we should know better than to save things by now. Is it for a celebration that we have saved the best for last, the filet mignon to be eaten after the last chemotherapy, to mark the moments when the neuropathy dissipates? My father volunteers to grill the meat, but *Oh, no*, I say fiercely, with such a look of disdain and horror that he raises his hands in surrender and grins. *Agnes will do it.* My mother, resting on the couch, gives me a look that is not quite sarcasm. Some call the filet the most boring cut of meat, as it does not have the character of muscles that receive more use. These filets are at room temperature, patted dry, and then lightly oiled. Agnes is too well seasoned to allow sticking, but the trick is not to touch the steak either: in the hiss and sputter, the magic of the Maillard reaction is turning amino acids and simple sugars on the surface of the steak into hundreds of brand-new molecules that continue to break down into still further compounds. Searing is not about sealing in juices. This is not caramelizing, which is based on sugar. This transformation is something else entirely.

The steak will release itself when it is ready, which is important to remember. The steak knows more than I do. My mother remembers her mother standing in front of the stove in her slip and apron on a Sunday morning, browning a roast before they left for church. Searing is chemistry, it's alchemy, it's magic I don't understand, the way I don't understand how oil polymerizes on the surface of my skillet to turn the cast iron more nonstick than Teflon, in the way that I don't understand how the chemical composition of my mother's chemotherapy attacks cancer cells in her body, but also is a fertilizer to grow crops where they have not been able to grow. I wonder about that moment when the steak hits the pan, the sear, that moment where two things that cannot coexist meet—the hot and the cold, the fire and the raw—and must change into something completely different. The sear on a steak, toast in the toaster, the browning of my favorite English roasties, even the magnificent crust of the cakes I make in this skillet, the tool my mother's doctor used to cauterize vessels during her hysterectomy, the fire to harm or heal, the flames in the gas fireplace that go nowhere, consuming and producing nothing.

After five minutes in that 500-degree oven, the filets rest on plates with their potatoes while I put the skillet back on the burner to deglaze with the dark tang of

Worcestershire sauce, enjoying the hiss of it as I scrape the pan with my flat-bottomed wooden spoon, hoping I can remember the flavors of the pan sauce of my favorite steak in my favorite dark tavern in Ohio. The liquid reduces immediately, quicker than I am ready for, and I add a bit of butter and stir as it melts and hope it tastes good, because I won't taste it. I must have faith. The grated Parmesan is ready to sprinkle on the finished steak. I turn away, ready to drizzle the sauce, and, forgetting myself, I reach back for the skillet's handle with my bare hand.

We can't go back to the way we were. This time will always be the burn scars on my hands, the white slices of knife slips. It may not hurt anymore, but we are marked.

61

YOU WILL FIND BRIGHT brass bells in nearly all cancer treatment centers across the country, a small moment
of ceremony to mark the transition of a cancer patient
from one place into the next. Perhaps it is the end of radiation, as one transitions into chemotherapy, or perhaps
it signals the end of all treatment and the return to a life
where one does not have to worry about platelet counts.
On the day of my mother's last chemotherapy, she rings
the bell we've walked by every time we visit, the brass eight
inches tall, inscribed with the name of the family who do-
nated it. The nurses and staff gather to watch my mother
proudly snap the clapper, three loud, sharp tones that echo
through the infusion center. They hug her, some with tears
in their eyes. She smiles.

A man in an orange shirt comes to investigate, peer-
ing at the bell as the room returns to quiet. He introduces
himself. It is his first time here. My mother listens patiently
to his story, even as I hear the tone of voice that G.'s doctor
used, that weirdly firm and compassionate register, because
I held my mother's hand the day her doctor told her the

same. Later, my mother says, *You don't really get names in there.
And you're more likely to talk about road construction than "what are you
in for?"* There are Homeric epics to be written in the spaces
between words in this place, in what cannot be said in response to *You have cancer.* What else is there to say beyond *I'm
so sorry—we know what awaits you.*

I marvel at the intimate details G. shares with a perfect
stranger, this man looking for anyone to understand that
even though you may have a supportive group of family and
friends, they'll never know what it's like to hear your doctor
say *cancer*, to feel like you are speaking a language nobody
can understand, what it feels like to have that port in your
chest, to feel the hair you are losing stick to your lips, to
know how cancer becomes invisible when hair grows back,
when scars heal, when what has happened inside your body
returns to quiet and people forget.

I picture G. in that bright orange shirt, the crew neck
stretched out as if he'd been tugging on it, filling the space
with his life story as my mother rings the bell. That was us,
six months ago, unsure, afraid, looking for the grounding
of human connection to make the transition to treatment
bearable. Maybe G. will tell the story of a woman he met on
his first day, a woman whose name he never caught, as she
rang the bell and then walked out the door.

62

MY FRIEND J. ASKED me to tell him a childhood story of wind and I told him of standing on the red cinder block retaining wall next to the garage when I was eight or nine, and watching the westernmost pine tree in the yard, the branches closest to the ground so still they could balance a bubble on the needles, but the very tops of the tree were fussing, as if they knew something we didn't. The sky was green and I could hear thunder, but where I stood was too still even to be called calm. I felt stalked, though I could not have articulated that as a child. I was in the presence of a predator. I stood motionless and watched the tree's top, recognizing for the first time what a storm smelled like.

It's hot today, the heat index over one hundred, and we close the house against it, the curtains, even ourselves, as if quiet will cause the heat to pass by unnoticed, the way I remember childhood days before air conditioning, closing the east side of the house in the morning and the west side in the afternoon. In the hungry quiet of this June morning, I don't know what to do now that my mother's chemo is over, the CT scans clear of cancer, but the absence still feels wrong, somehow. I am suspicious of this calm, as I will be every three months as we wait for the results of her CT scans, waiting for the storm I know must lurk beyond the stillness. I struggle against this frozen moment that still feels like *waiting*, the expectation that we will carry on as if the last six months never happened, the release of the tension so abrupt as to be disorienting. We have held tight for so long.

Anyone who's been through an illness like cancer knows there's a point where everything contracts, pulls in like blood to the core, away from the limbs, into the empty space in my mother's abdomen where her uterus with its three-pound embryonal rhabdomyosarcoma tumor used to be. Language becomes predatory. Fingers become superfluous, the need for circulation to the knees, gone. The body becomes a fist. This is how we survive: We don't struggle. We still. My mother has no detectable cancer, but we still worry about those cancer seeds, waiting in the stillness to replant themselves.

63

JUNE IS THE RETURN of childhood memories of standing with my mother and sisters in the cool darkness of the seed store in Park Rapids for beans and radishes and carrots that we will plant in our backyard, the preparation of food to replenish our freezer shelves emptied over the winter. My mother will give us each our own rows and my sisters and I will get to choose what we want to plant in them, the same way my brother-in-law does with my niece in their small backyard plot. I remember how tiny the carrot seeds were and I remember how my mother would give us the choice of which vegetable we wanted for dinner on those dark winter nights, the carrots disappearing first, then the green beans, to be left with the beets and squash that none of the three of us liked. I think differently of seeds now. Now they are what my mother's doctors are vigilantly searching for on those CT scans that she undergoes every three months, hoping to catch any new tumors small before they spread like vines on the back of the garden. A lot can happen in three months: my mother went from cancer free to a cabbage-sized tumor in three months; we watched the fear of miscarriage lessen as my sister crossed from her first trimester into her second; in August, they will welcome a child who will number three.

64

AT OUR FAMILY'S HOMEPLACE, my grandparents'
Cabin on Third Crow Wing Lake, the place that holds my
heart, I walk down to the lake in the quiet of a morning
that knows more than we do, the loons warbling and then
growing silent against the darkness of the west that rumbles
with the promise of a morning thunderstorm. There is incredible stillness here, leaves frozen, not even the chitter
of squirrels. In the green under my feet, a spot of red is
hiding in the shapes of leaves I recognize: wild strawberries. June is strawberry season in Hubbard County. Our
winter cardinal has given way to the red of fruit. Strawberries are the only fruit with its seeds on the outside, each
one averaging, we are told, two hundred seeds. A seed of
memory sprouts, then: my grandmother trying to occupy
three little girls by hunting for tiny wild strawberries down
by the lake, a hunt that never yielded more than six or eight
strawberries that never had enough surface area to be more
than a mouthful of seeds, but a treasure always requiring
two scoops of ice cream to celebrate. Is this what happens
when an internal moment becomes external, the moment

where I am called to pause in stillness that smells faintly of fear and anticipation and joy—is the point of this moment not the blister of ozone, not the fear of what seeds will grow with the rain from this storm, but the bright burst of a wild strawberry, the tart and the sweet, the way it's supposed to be, fresh, as the storm moves on?

Works Referenced

Ackerman, Diane. *A Natural History of the Senses*. New York: Vintage Books, 1995.

"Cancer Cells and Chemotherapy." Chemocare. https://chemocare.com/chemotherapy/what-is-chemotherapy/cancer-cells-chemotherapy.aspx.

Donoghue, Denis. "Disease Should Be Itself," review of *Illness as Metaphor*, by Susan Sontag. *New York Times* (July 16, 1978). https://archive.nytimes.com/www.nytimes.com/books/00/03/12/specials/sontag-illness.html.

Erdrich, Heid E. "Microchimerism." In *Cell Traffic: New and Selected Poems*. Tucson: University of Arizona Press, 2012.

Lewis, C. S. *A Grief Observed*. New York: Harper One, 1961.

Lowell, James Russell. "The First Snowfall." In *Journeys through Bookland: A New and Original Plan for Reading Applied to the*

World's Best Literature for Children, vol. 2, edited by Charles H. Sylvester. Chicago: Bellows-Reeve Company, 1922.

Martone, Robert. "Scientists Discover Children's Cells Living in Mothers' Brains." *Scientific American*, December 4, 2012. https://www.scientificamerican.com/article/scientists-discover-childrens-cells-living-in-mothers-brain/.

Purpura, Lia. "On Miniatures." *Brevity* 21 (Summer 2006). https://www.creativenonfiction.org/brevity/craft/craft_minis.htm.

Sontag, Susan. "Illness as Metaphor." In *Illness as Metaphor and AIDS and Its Metaphors*. London: Penguin Books, 1996.

Synge, John Millington. *The Aran Islands*. Boston: John W. Luce & Company, 1911.

Yeats, William Butler. "Aedh Wishes for the Cloths of Heaven." In *The Wind among the Reeds*. London: Elkin Mathews, 1903.

Acknowledgments

This book bears many levels of gratitude. First, to my mother and father, to my sisters Kristi and Kim, my brother-in-law Mike, to the niblings, Cora, Henry, and Sam: this book would not exist without you. You are my everything.

For those who are mentioned here only by initials, because theirs is not my story to tell. For M., F., A., S., L., my mother's sisters in strength.

Thank you to Lynne Osterman and the Babine Belly Brigade for keeping us fed when we could not do it ourselves.

Thank you to Dr. Derek Johnson, Amanda Castillon, Dr. Drew Rosielle, and Kaitlyn McMullen.

Thank you to the readers on this book and its pieces, especially Renée D'Aoust, Karen Craigo, Scott Olsen, Jonathan Johnson, and Jim Rogers. I am grateful to Patrick Swaney and Claire Eder at *Quarter After Eight*, W. Scott Olsen at *Ascent*, Bryan Fry at *Blood Orange Review*, Ira Sukrungruang at

Sweet, Jeremy Schraffenberger at *North American Review*, Ander Monson and Nicole Walker at *DIAGRAM*, Amy Wright at *Zone 3*, Crystal Gibbins at *Split Rock Review*, Matt Weinkam at *Passages North*, Dinty Moore at *Brevity*, Donna Talarico at *Hippocampus*, Emily Johnson at *Blue Earth Review*, Steven Church at the *Normal School*, and Allison Joseph and Jon Tribble at *Crab Orchard Review*, for believing in the pieces that make up this project. I am incredibly grateful to my editor, Daniel Slager, for his incredible vision and unfailing support.

Brandi Ashman

KAREN BABINE is the author of *Water and What We Know: Following the Roots of a Northern Life*, winner of the 2016 Minnesota Book Award for memoir/creative nonfiction and a finalist for the Midwest Book Award and the Northeastern Minnesota Book Award. She also edits *Assay: A Journal of Nonfiction Studies*. She holds an MFA in creative nonfiction from Eastern Washington University and a PhD in English from the University of Nebraska-Lincoln. She lives in Minnesota.

Founded as a nonprofit organization in 1980, Milkweed
Editions is an independent publisher. Our mission is to
identify, nurture and publish transformative literature,
and build an engaged community around it.

milkweed.org

Interior design by Mary Austin Speaker

Typeset in Mrs Eaves

by Mary Austin Speaker

Mrs Eaves is a transitional typeface designed by
Zuzana Licko in 1996 for Emigre and was named
after Sarah Eaves, the wife of famed typographer
John Baskerville.